My Story

Malcolm Trayhorn

Published by Paragon Publishing

© Malcolm Trayhorn 2021

ISBN 978-1-78222-818-9

Book design, layout and production management by Into Print
www.intoprint.net, +44 (0)1604 832140

Foreword

Where to start? If this is to be a reflection and remembered account of my whole life then I can't really start from when I was born as I really can't remember that! Can anybody?

Probably the best thing I can do as a suitable compromise is to give a brief account of where I came from. This means telling you about my parents and although both now deceased were both contributors to my existence.

Chapter 1 – Parents

My Father:

Eric Arthur Trayhorn was Born 16th June 1924 in Ponders End and was the 5th of 6 children. He attended Alma Road School, Enfield until the age of 14 when he left to start work at Co-op grocery shops in Lincoln Road and then Hertford Road, Enfield. From there he went to work in the Co-op Bakery, Ordnance Road, Enfield where he used to do a delivery round.

The Co-op also had offices in Ordnance Road and a young girl who worked there used to go to the Bakery to get cakes and met the young Eric. She of course was Doreen Rose Odell (Mum) aged 16.

Dad was called up into the Army on 3rd November 1942 aged only 18. He broke off his courtship at that time being uncertain of his future and went off to War. He joined the Royal Army Service Corps – Private 14324392. There he quickly made his mark and within 2 years reached the rank of sergeant. He was involved in the D Day landings and was part of the liberating forces that landed on Gold beach. I can't begin to imagine the mixture of fear, exhilaration and sheer terror that an 18-year-old must go through, or the sights and experiences that have to be endured.

He was classified as a driver and qualified to drive the large Foden lorries that carried pipes for Operation PLUTO. [This was Pipe Line Under The Ocean and was key to supplying petrol in support of Operation Overlord, the Allied invasion of Normandy. Fuel was pumped from England via the pipeline laid firstly under the English Channel and subsequently on land.] Dad would drive the lorry carrying the pipes and the Engineers would offload and lay them across land.

He must have been a trusted driver as he also drove staff cars with high ranking officers as passengers. This required him to check the cars inside and out for explosive devices before anyone entered the vehicle.

A part of this process apparently required the bouncing up and down on the rear seats. Later he was given the responsibility of running one of the petrol stations along the pipeline and was in charge of a large number of men. For years he never really spoke of his experiences in the army but in later years was taken to telling some of his exploits, too many to impart here.

One that haunted him was an occasion when a convoy he was travelling with had stopped as they came under attack and Dad was positioned at the side of the road with his gun. Apparently, an officer came along and told Dad to swap places with another soldier for some reason and a short time later the position he had been in took a direct hit and the soldier there was blown up. Dad told that he had the job of helping to bury this soldier and always said that it felt like he was burying himself.

He was released from the army in May of 1947. In his release book his captain wrote, "This NCO has had considerable all-round driving experience, has also experience of office work and supervision. He has showed considerable drive and initiative, is industrious and conscientious in his work." His service was shown as exemplary.

At the end of the war he went back to work for the Co-op at Bush Hill Park and returned to Ordnance Road where he waited outside the Co-op offices for the young girl left behind over 2 years previously. They courted for 4 months, got engaged and 4 months later on 1st June 1946 they were married.

My Sister, Moira Anita was born on 27th July 1949 and in 1951 they moved to Holmesdale where they stayed. I appeared on the scene soon after on 13th August 1951. After 13 years my Brother Barry Edward was next to arrive on 20th October 1964 and 2 years later another sister Janine Doreen was the last on 5th April 1966.

Until his later years Dad was a very active man and was involved in many activities and local matters. He always kept his large garden well stocked with vegetables and also had allotments nearby. An early one of these was on the field in front of the house (now the top of the Holmesdale tunnel on the M25 motorway). He could turn his hand to most things and built much of the furniture and fittings in the house. He loved to tinker about in his shed and was always building something out of rescued bits of timber. Wendy houses, Bird boxes, toy castles, toy garages, stalls and games for use at fetes.

He worked at Arthur Griggs Grocery store in Chase Side for a number of years. I remember visiting the shop as a small boy and especially the delightful aroma of freshly ground coffee beans and wonderous sights of all the tins of biscuits and other groceries. He left there after false promises made to him by the owner. As well as his full-time job he also worked in the evenings and weekends every Christmas at a local butcher, plucking and preparing poultry. Later he used to help out at weekends at a Farm doing general labouring work.

From the Grocery shop he went to work for Don Gresswells, booksellers also in Chase Side. He was with them for a number of years and later transferred firstly to new premises at Grange Park and then Plumpton Road, Hoddesdon. He took early retirement from there after again being let down by the management.

Dad was an active member of St George's Residents Association and involved himself in the road infrastructure in the area. Indeed, his expertise and knowledge were recognised as the prospective local Member of Parliament, Tim Eggar, approached him to find out the issues and used to consult with Dad regularly. It may not be a well-known fact but Dad was instrumental, together with another resident in preventing the M25 cutting through the ground in front of our house as a flyover, which was the original plan. As a result of much campaigning the Holmesdale tunnel was designed and constructed.

He also had connections with the disabled and the elderly. He would attend and assist at a day centre in Brimsdown and helped with riding for the disabled. I visited my parents at least once a week, usually on a Friday, when I would have a chat with him about what I had been up to. He was very proud of the fact that I had joined the police and used to say that he would love to have joined when he was younger. Dad suffered a heart attack at the age of 62. He had 5 operations on his left hip, which eventually was fused and left him unable to get about. His last years were spent in a reclining chair watching his telly.

Both of my Sisters were really good at caring for both parents and Moira in particular would take Dad to Hospital and Doctors' appointments as well as helping with his needs. I can't honestly say that I was close to my Father, he wasn't one to go to the pub with you for a pint nor was he very sociable. He was not able to cope with crowds or noisy places. In his later years I was regretfully not as compassionate or supportive as I should have been. He had not had an easy life and undoubtedly suffered from Post-Traumatic Stress Disorder. I wish I had spent more time with him in those last years and been more tolerant and understanding. Since he passed away it has taught me to value everyone and especially those close to me. Whenever I hear the Luther Vandross song, 'Dance with my Father' it makes me think... *'How I'd love love love to speak with my Father again.'*

My Father died in Chase Farm Hospital in 2013, following a burst aortic aneurism aged 88. My Mum, Sisters, Brother and myself were with him at the Hospital during his final hours. He always said that he was proud of his ENTIRE family, his Children, Grandchildren and Great Grandchildren and all that they had achieved. He was most of all very appreciative of Mum's love and support (He always called her Doll) and I could always hear him thanking her for what she did for him and saying, "I love you Darling". I don't really know how you can consolidate 88 years of someone's life into a few short paragraphs but hopefully this gives a brief glimpse of Eric Arthur Trayhorn, Husband, Father of 4, Grandfather of 11 and Great Grandfather of 7.

My Mother:

Doreen Rose Odell was born on 31st July 1926 in Edmonton. She was one of 3 children to Rose Lydia and Harry Odell. She had two older brothers, Albert Francis Mons and Kenneth James. She attended Edmonton High Grade school, was a keen student who got on well with everyone.

Her Father, Harry, was tragically killed in a bicycle accident in Edmonton in 1933 at the age of 45. Her Mother subsequently met and married George Hawkins, affectionately referred to as *"Pops"*. They lived for many years at Countisbury Avenue, Bush Hill Park, Enfield.

After leaving School she went to work in the Co-op Offices in Ordnance Road, Enfield. Whilst working there she used to go to the Bakery to get cakes and met the 18-year-old Eric Arthur Trayhorn who worked there; she was 16. They began courting and she was introduced into the wider Trayhorn clan of Dad's Brothers and Sisters. Mum became friendly with his Brother Frank's girl, Margaret and his Sister Molly especially and Mum always recalled the times during the war when they would go out dancing. She would also meet up with her Brother Ken when he was home on leave from the Royal Navy. Sadly, Kenneth was killed on 13th December 1944 at the age of 21 during action towards the end of the Second World War. My middle name is Kenneth, which was given to me in memory of my Uncle.

As already mentioned, when Dad was called up into the Army on 3rd November 1942 aged only 18, he broke off his courtship, being uncertain of his future and went off to war. At the end of the war he went back to work for the Co-op at Bush Hill Park and returned to Ordnance Road where he waited outside the Co-op offices for the young girl left behind over 2 years previously. They courted for 4 months, got engaged and 4 months later on 1st June 1946 they were married. Not having any money, they moved in with Nanny Hawkins at Countisbury Avenue where they lived for the first years of their marriage.

As with most families at that time they struggled to make ends meet and Mum played a significant role in running the home and providing for Moira and me. Mum worked in the School Kitchens, something that she did for many years at different schools. She also worked for John West Catering as a Silver Service waitress for 35 years, a job she continued until she was 75. She loved meeting up with all the John West gang at weddings and functions where she worked. She always had tales to tell of the different houses and places she got to visit and the laughs they all had.

Mum enjoyed many things, including, cake making, cake decorating (especially sugar craft), keep fit classes, Women's Guild, a game of bowls, Christmases and Boxing days with the family gathered round, playing games with the Grandchildren, plying people with tea and cakes and sandwiches and salad and biscuits and trifle and… well you get the picture.

My Mother loved to laugh and have a good time. She liked nothing better than to get up and have a dance at any function. Over the years I recall her getting up to have a jig around and did not think people were having a good time unless they were up dancing. She loved to listen to military bands and was also fond of Andre Rieu and his Orchestra. Moira took her to see him and his orchestra in concert at the Albert Hall and she didn't stop speaking about it. She was fairly adept at playing the piano and would often sit down to play. This was especially so at Christmas when we would gather round the piano to sing carols whilst Mum played. She took this up at an early age and would accompany our Grandmother, (Mum's Mum) whilst she sang. A favourite was always The Rose of Tralee as Rose was her name as well as being Mum's middle name.

Mum did have her funny little quirks; She would often mispronounce words such as...

Cappachini instead of Cappuccino, *Gozabo* instead of Gazebo, *Osopholos* instead of Oesophagus, *Cinchani & lemolade* instead of Cinzano & Lemonade and *Stella & Tony* instead of Stella Artois.

My Father was the love of her life and her dedication and love for him remained until his death in 2013. Since he passed away she was very lonely and pined for him and would say, "Why did he go and leave me". She was a devoted Wife of Eric for over 66 years.

My Sisters were very good at looking after Mum when Dad passed away as she felt very isolated at home on her own. Although I did do my bit towards looking after her it was undoubtedly the two girls who did the lions share. Being the first boy, I was not able to do anything wrong in Mum's eyes. My sisters both said that I was the blue-eyed boy and they received little praise for their efforts whereas it was always, 'My Malcolm this and my Malcolm that'. Did I feel guilty? No. She was getting more and more frail but was very independent and did not want to end up in a care home. I would phone regularly and every Friday would take her shopping in Waltham Cross. She always looked forward to this and before we started shopping we would have a cup of tea and a cake in the shopping pavilion café. This gave her the opportunity to watch other people and have a chat with any passing friends. I would then take her round to the bank where she would withdraw £200 (which she never needed really). Then she would go into Sainsburys to get her shopping. I would follow behind with the trolley while she picked out her shopping items. The problem was that she still thought she was shopping for a family and put the same items in each week, whether she needed them or not. First stop was the fruit and veg. where she put in tomatoes, a cucumber, a lettuce, greens, a cauliflower, runner beans, apples, oranges and strawberries, to name but a few. This pattern followed in all the other sections and aisles. Anything that had a special offer would be put in the trolley. Toilet rolls were a must as well as tins of salmon (I actually found over 20 tins in her larder one day whilst checking dates on her collection of tins). I found the best way of preventing waste and reducing her bill was to put things back on the shelf when she wasn't looking. The staff in the supermarket knew Mum well and when they saw me trying to return items they would say, "Here give it to me I'll put it back for you." The amazing thing was that she never suspected or found out what I was doing even when we reached the check-out and unloaded the trolley. I did get caught out once, however. I got a phone call one day when she wanted to know where the strawberries were that she had put in the trolley. My Brother and his family had turned up unexpectedly for tea and she wanted to give them strawberries for a desert. I quickly purchased some strawberries and took them round to her, telling her that they must have fallen out of her bag into the boot of the car. I know! What a terrible son!

My Sister, Moira, went to the house to visit her on 10th June 2015 and found her lying on the kitchen floor. She phoned me, after phoning for an ambulance and I went straight round. I believe she was trying to lock up the back door and stretched up to reach the top lock, causing her to collapse. She still had the key in her hand but had been dead for some hours before being discovered. Her Doctor attended and signed a death certificate giving cause of death as Congestive Cardiac failure, Ischaemic Heart Disease and Hypertensions. She loved all of her 4 Children, 11 Grandchildren and 7 Great Grandchildren. She was a lovely lady, very much loved and sadly missed.

Chapter 2 – My Beginnings

So, after a brief outline of my parents I will go on to tell my story.

Mum and Dad moved into a new house in 1951 not long before I was born. It was an end of terrace 3-bedroom house in Holmesdale. Although the postal address was Waltham Cross, Hertfordshire, it was actually just over the border in Middlesex. This meant that I went to school in Enfield, starting off at Suffolks infants' school. I have very few memories of this school but remember that Mum worked there as a dinner lady. I do remember that a new primary school had been built in Bullsmoor Lane and as this was nearer to our home so my Sister Moira and I were transferred there. This was Capel Manor and I remained there happily until leaving to go to secondary school. I remember that the Head Mistress was Scottish and therefore she introduced a regime of Scottish Country dancing. This was my first venture into anything in the entertainment line and must have shown some aptitude as I performed publicly representing the school in the country dancing team. I must have been about eight years old. More about my would-be entertainer desires later, as it crops up several times during my story.

Nothing much else of interest happened during those school years really. I do however remember the long trek backwards and forwards to school over, 'the hill' and across the busy A10 main arterial road. In those days it was a crossroads controlled by traffic lights and was single carriageway in each direction. Later a roundabout replaced the traffic lights, but it has now reverted back to a traffic light-controlled junction once again and the A10 is now a dual carriageway in each direction. There was a sweet shop situated on the junction side of the hill so we used to stop on the way home to get sweets to help us on the long walk over the hill. It seemed like a really long way then but in reality, it was only a few hundred yards. Our budget at the sweet shop was three old pennies (equivalent in decimal terms is 1¼ pence). With this one could buy 4 black jacks, 4 fruit salads, 2 sherbet flying saucers or a toffee chew bar for one penny, a sherbet fountain for tuppence (two pennies) or even a jamboree bag for the whole thruppence (three pennies). Inside this would be a few sweets and a surprise toy, a sort of early day Kinder surprise. Sometimes on a Wednesday my Dad would appear after school to give me a crossbar home on his bike, which was propelled by a small petrol driven motor attached to the back wheel. It was his half day from the grocer's shop and it was a great treat.

Holmesdale was a quiet road in the 50's and 60's, especially at, "our end", which only had 10 houses (two terraces of 5 houses). It was a dead end as there were nurseries with green houses stretching as far as the eye could see after the last house. If we were feeling mischievous, we would lob stones over the high hedge separating the field from the glasshouses and await the sound of breaking glass. In front of the houses there was a stretch of land that had not been built on and we used to call it, 'the wilderness' or just, 'the field'. Nobody really knew then why it had been left vacant but we didn't care as it was a great playground. It turned out years later that it had been left vacant because the planned London Orbital Motorway (M25) was to come through here.

As many families had moved in around the same time, we knew most of the people along the street. First house was the Connel's, then the Everton's, the Ayrton's, the Gladdens, the Goodchild's, us, the Fosters, the Hempstead's, the Newman's and the Clarkes. Growing up in Holmesdale was great, there was always something going on. My play chums were mostly Andrew, Paula, Timothy, Stephen and John as we were all of a similar age. We would spend hours playing along the back alley or on the field in front of the houses.

One game we played was making our way around the far reaches and overgrown areas of the field by way of upturned milk crates. These were obtained from the pile of metal crates stockpiled in Holmesdale by the milkman, who used to stack them on the corner of the road. The milk company was called Warner's and they had a horse and cart that was used to deliver milk to local customers. The corner was where he would stop for a break, stack empty crates and feed the horse.

Getting back to our game, we would each have a crate, which we would upturn and place in front of us and then stand on it, one behind the other. There would be one spare crate that would be passed up to the front person who would put it in front and then step forward onto it. Everyone would then move forward until the spare crate appeared behind the last person. That person would pass it forward and so on. The person in front decided the route but it was usually through the places where there were overgrown stinging nettles and log grass. For those with short trousers or skirts, which was everyone, there was the risk of getting stung, so being nearby to a dock leaf was handy so that you could rub your legs to relieve the pain.

Another game we loved to play was, 'Outings'. One person would be 'IT' and have to stand by a garden wall designated as 'Home'. Everyone else had to the count of 100 to run and hide whilst the person at home closed their eyes. That person would then shout, "Coming ready or not" and then set off to find the rest. If someone was spotted the person spotting had to get back to home before the spotted person and shout, "Forty Forty I see John" or whoever. If successful that person was captured and had to remain at 'Home'. If you could get back to' Home' before the seeker and shout, "Ally Ally out", then any people at 'Home' would be released to go off and hide again. It was not a popular position to be 'IT', you could be there for ages.

Other games played were, marbles, cigarette card flicking, skipping with a large rope, jacks, hula hoops and hopscotch, to name but a few. I remember clearly that we used to meet up in each other's sheds, especially on rainy days, to play board games. Monopoly was usually the game of choice and we would play for hours. Paula and I were the main participants and the two of us were regularly together round a monopoly board. We took out the chance cards that related to taxes on houses owned as we didn't really understand them. I was always the dog and Paula was always the ship.

Over the following years I spent a lot of time with Paula. We used to go to London on rover tickets, visiting museums and the tourist sights. I recall on one outing we were on the tube when I got a nose bleed (something that I have always suffered with and still do to this day). On this occasion it persisted and passengers on the train became concerned. One gave me a handkerchief as mine was soaked with blood and another suggested that I make my way to a London Hospital. We did make our way to a casualty department at a Hospital and true to form, as soon as we arrived the flow of blood ceased.

I would go with her and her parents for days out and I would visit when they moved house later on. I have to say that I had strong feelings for her and both sets of parents said it would be unsurprising if we ended up together. However, circumstances intervened with us going different directions and the fact that she actually preferred girls rather than boys. Christmas cards and birthday cards are still wending their way backwards and forwards and Monopoly gets mentioned quite often. Paula is very clever and talented, she went on to become a skilled ocularist, making and fitting prosthetic eyes for people throughout the world.

I remember quite clearly the bonfire nights we had during those years and preparations began weeks before the night itself. A Guy would be fashioned from some old clothing (usually a pair of my Dad's old trousers and shirt). The arms and legs would be Mum's old stockings stuffed with scrunched up newspapers. With a face painted on another stuffed stocking rounded to make a head it would be stitched up and a hat shoved on top. We would put it in an old pram or pushchair and wheel it into Waltham Cross where we would shout, "Penny for the Guy." The middle of 'The Field' was used to build a bonfire, for which everyone contributed. We would call at houses all along the surrounding streets with a wheelbarrow, to ask if people had anything they wanted burned. Any old furniture, bits of wood or rubbish was added to the pile until it reached epic proportions. I seem to remember that old runner bean plants were very good for burning as the beans had finished by then and the left-over vegetation was dry and a great addition. One year a rival group set fire to our bonfire prior to the night so thereafter we mounted a guard to protect it until the night. The only thing that prevented the fireworks or the lighting the bonfire on the 5th November was if it fell on a Sunday. Such an event on a Sunday was a definite no-no. Everyone down the street would come out with their fireworks and after the bonfire was ignited, they were enjoyed by all. The Mums would come out with crispy skinned baked potatoes and piping hot sausages in a roll, which were shared around. It was a great occasion and it was rare that you would hear any fireworks going off any other nights before or after the day. Nowadays firework nights seem to go on for days and even weeks before and after the 5th.

A favourite thing was to obtain an old set of pram wheels, a plank of wood, some odd bits of wood and a bolt which, when put together properly, turned into a desirable form of transport known as a trolley. We would have races along the back alley with one person sitting on the trolley using their feet to steer whilst someone else pushed, usually with a stick or old broom handle. You could also sit with your back to the driver and push with your feet with a backwards running motion, that way you were both getting a ride. A clever and experienced rider could manage to ride the trolley by kneeling on it and steering with a piece of rope whilst scooting with the other foot. I have a picture of me doing just this along the road at the front of our house. In the early days we didn't have to worry too much about cars as nobody down the street owned one. In fact, my Father was the first one to have a vehicle and that was the grocers van that he was allowed to use to get backwards and forwards to work. We never got to go out in it however, as he wasn't allowed to use it for his own purposes. Later my Father was the only one down the street who didn't own a vehicle of his own!

My friend Stephen's Dad was a London black cab driver and a lovely kind man who spoiled Stephen and all of us kids down the road. Although they lived just round the corner, on firework night he would always turn up with bags full of fireworks for everyone to share. On Sunday mornings, as soon as the weather was reasonable, he would take a few of us in his cab to the large open-air swimming pool in Enfield. This was not a heated pool and was always freezing cold. However, this was where I learned to swim and gain my confidence in the water. Stephen's Dad, Bill, would swim the whole length of the pool underwater and as it was a huge pool this was considered an incredible achievement. After we got changed to go home, we would get a mug of hot water with an oxo cube crushed up in it to warm us up. Then each year at Christmas time he would take us to the London Palladium to see the pantomime. I remember Charlie Drake and Norman Wisdom in particular. It was always a very exciting treat and I will always remember Bill and his kindness.

Christmas was a magical time and I remember waking up on

Christmas morning and scampering to the foot of the bed to see what was in the stocking that I had put there the night before. When I say stocking, it actually was. One of Mum's old ones. Inside there would be walnuts, almonds, a tangerine, a beano annual, a Mars selection stocking and another small gift such as a torch. I would tuck into the tangerine and read my beano under the bed covers using the torch until there were signs of movement from my Sister's room. We would then creep downstairs to see if, 'He' had been. There was a curtain between the living room and the front room, where the tree and presents were waiting in the darkness. A peep through the curtain confirmed that, 'He' had indeed been, but we were not allowed into the front room until we had eaten a hearty breakfast. I seem to remember that we would chomp our way through eggs, bacon and fried bread for breakfast, a full roast turkey dinner with all the trimmings at lunchtime and then a full salad style spread for tea time. What wonderful times and something that I tried to replicate for my Children and Grandchildren. Now that they are all either grown up or growing up, I relive the magic by playing Father Christmas professionally, but more about this later. Nowadays, however it is a croissant and Bucks fizz for breakfast, the full roast turkey dinner late in the afternoon and a sandwich for supper.

My Sister, Moira, who is two years older than me, and I would argue quite a lot as I remember. Mum would threaten us with, "I'm telling your Father when he gets home", or reach for the cane that was kept over the kitchen door frame. When I was thirteen, I remember that Moira and I were at home waiting for Mum and Dad to come back from the Doctors. Little did we realise the reason until it was disclosed that we were to have a baby Brother or Sister. How did that happen? I certainly was not aware of the process. No one had explained the birds and bees to me and sex education was not something that was discussed. Well I gained a baby Brother, Barry, at the age of thirteen and as if that was not shocking enough a baby Sister, Janine, two years later!

Waltham Cross was a short walk from our house across 'The Field' and through the council estate. There were two cinemas there, the Regent, more commonly referred to as the flea pit, and the Embassy. The Embassy was much larger and had a balcony. It was rare to get a seat in the balcony as it was more expensive. I would go with others on a Saturday morning to the Embassy for, surprisingly enough, Saturday morning pictures. It was a tanner (sixpence) to get in downstairs and if you were flush with cash ninepence upstairs. The programme would start off with the organ ascending from the front area and familiar tunes being played. All the kids in the cinema would sing at the top of their voices and it would always finish off with a rousing chorus of Davey Crocket king of the wild frontier. There would be a feature film, usually a cowboy, this was followed by a cartoon and then the serial, Batman & Robin or Buck Rogers. If you were particularly well off you could get a Mivi for sixpence but much more important was a bag of chips on the way home, again for sixpence. Perhaps even a large pickled onion or a wally for a penny.

Other early memories of Waltham Cross were; Marsden's, which was where you went to get your records. They had a number of listening booths and you would ask the person behind the counter if they would play your potential choice and they would nominate a booth and play the record. This was a sort of try before you buy but generally just a cheap way of listening to your favourite record of the day. If you did decide to buy a single 45rpm record the cost was one and sixpence (7 ½ pence in new money). I would get Half a Crown (two and sixpence) (12 ½ pence) pocket money, so buying a record would put a significant dent in my budget. I had an electric train set so was keen to buy pieces of track or rolling stock for that. Asplands was the shop for this and in the upstairs toy department I could buy one piece of track for one and thruppence, which was half my pocket money. Woolworths was always a shop to visit and look at all the counter displays, especially the pick and mix sweets and the toy counter.

I collected the Airfix toy soldier sets that were small figures inside a box and contained a number of soldiers in different poses. The Afrika Korps, British 8th Army, German Infantry, British Infantry, US Marines and the Japanese Infantry were sets I collected and with which I fought out many battles on the living room carpet.

Very few people had phones in their houses, we certainly didn't, so if you needed to make a call you had to go to the nearest phone box. Our nearest one was about a quarter of a mile away at the junction of Bullsmoor Lane and Hertford Road. It was situated on a triangular piece of ground surrounded on all sides by busy roads and next to a horse trough. Once the box was free, and you hoped that if there was someone making a call or there was a queue that they weren't making a long call. Once in the box you put your fourpence in the money slot and dialled the number you wanted. When someone answered you pressed button A to be able to speak. The money dropped into the box at the bottom. If no-one answered you pressed button B and your fourpence would be returned.

I do remember that we would travel along the Hertford Road on a trolley bus until they were replaced by motor buses in 1961. The overhead wires ran all the way along the road from Edmonton Tramway Avenue to Waltham Cross. On one occasion before Barry and Janine came on the scene, our Grandma Hawkins took me and Moira to the Co-op in Enfield Wash to buy us our first record player. I believe it was a Dansette or something very similar. We were allowed to get one record to play on it when we got home. Moira chose "Little Sister" by Elvis Presley and mine (don't laugh) was "My boomerang won't come back" by Charlie Drake.

Grandma Hawkins lived in Bush Hill Park and was my Mum's Mum. We spent many times waiting at bus stops to get a bus to Edmonton. Either a 217-red bus, which took you the whole distance or a 310 green bus which took you to Southbury Road, Enfield where you changed to get a red bus for the rest of the way. At the other end there was what seemed like a real trek to get to the house. On the way back, if we were lucky, we would stop at the off-licence near the bus stop and get a bag of Smith's crisps. Inside there was a little blue paper twist which contained salt. When untwisted you tipped it into the bag and shook it. I think they tasted better than ones you get now!

I remember that if we went shopping with her in Edmonton, we would go into Bernde's fish shop where she would ask to see the eels. A tray full of live eels would be brought in from the back of the shop all wriggling around and over each other. Grandma would point to one or two which were extricated with great skill by the fishmonger placed on a wooden slab where their heads were duly despatched from their bodies. When we got back to her house, she would chop them up, cook them and serve them up with plenty of mash potato and lashings of parsley sauce a chunk of bread and a dose of vinegar. Sometimes by way of a change we would have cockles, whelks or winkles which we ate in front of an open fire using a hatpin to get the winkle from its shell. What memorable treats, however you wouldn't see me within a mile of any of those delicacies now!

As my Father was one of six, I had lots of cousins. Uncle Frank and Aunty Margaret lived in Waltham Cross and we spent a great Christmas there. I remember sleeping over and being in the same bed with cousin Bob and cousin Jimmy. I think it was during that stay that I had my first experience of a milk shake, which was made in a blender with ice cream, strawberry juice and milk. It was magical, I can still taste it now.

One Summer we went to visit Uncle Charlie and Aunty Doris in Ascot. I thought they were very posh and I was expected to be on my best behaviour. Another taste first for me was Colman's ready mixed mustard which was spread on a ham sandwich we had for lunch there. I absolutely loved it and to this day I have it with most dinners or sandwiches with any meat. I get through pots of the stuff and no other mustard comes anywhere near for me.

A favourite Uncle for me was Uncle Ted who used to visit us with Aunty Pat from High Wycombe. He always gave me half a crown when he left, a small fortune (12 ½ pence in new money) no wonder he was my favourite. I have done the same for my nieces and nephews over the years they have been growing up, slipping them a pound as I shook their hand when saying goodbye. All thanks to Uncle Ted. A couple of summers I was taken back to High Wycombe to spend a week at their house with cousin Jimmy. Uncle Ted worked in a butcher's shop and I remember that as well as having breakfast, dinner and tea we always had chipolata sausages for supper. I did look forward to that week!

At this point I need to confess to my criminal past. Mum would trust me to get shopping for her at Key Markets store in the 'Cross' (Waltham Cross). One day I was in there passing the chocolate and I plead guilty to having slipped a bar into my pocket and leaving without paying for it. It was easy, so I repeated this again and again, hiding my stash under my bed. However, my life of crime was curtailed when I was stopped outside one day and taken into the office. I can't tell you how scared I was, mostly about Mum and Dad being called. It was much to my relief that the manager just threatened to do this if he ever saw me in his shop again. I didn't go back in there again for a long time and never stole anything again from that day to this. My Mum and Dad never knew about my fall from the straight and narrow and I'm sure she must have wondered why any shopping was then got from Victor Values or Payantakes as opposed to Key Markets.

Our back garden was quite long and split into two with a path splitting the first section through the middle of two lawns and then running along the edge of the second section. This section was Dad's vegetable patch where he would grow potatoes and all manner of vegetables. We had a clockwork train set that Dad got from somewhere. It had a suitcase full of track and when put together it would stretch from the back door all the way down the path to the back alley. The clockwork train was a large green one with six wheels and a set of bogie wheels at the front. It had a coal tender truck behind and would get all the way to the end of the garden and most of the way back on just one wind up. It had levers in the cab part that operated it going forward or backwards and a switch underneath that when it hit a particular track at the end of the line would switch it from forward to backwards. I don't know what happened to it but I bet it would have been worth a fortune now! Another thing we got up to in the back alley was darts. A dart board was set up of the back of our shed and we would play for hours with some Dads joining in. Dad also got hold of a half sized slate based snooker table from somewhere and this was set up in the garden. It wasn't in the best condition but we had some great times playing on it. I can't remember where we stored it or what happened to it.

Holidays were few but Moira and I particularly remember Great stones, Little Dinham caravan Holiday Park in Cornwall and Leysdown on the Isle of Sheppey. We also had day outings on the train to Southend with Mums and kids from Holmesdale. We would all walk to the rail station in Waltham Cross full of excitement for the day to come and carrying our buckets and spades. First a train into London Liverpool Street and then finding the correct platform for the train to Southend. The journey time was around two hours if you got good connections but it seemed like hours to us. If we were lucky, we would manage to get a carriage to ourselves so that we could hang out the window to experience the rush of wind in our faces. You would have to duck back in quickly if a tunnel was coming up and shut the window to stop the smut coming in from the engine's steam. On arrival at Southend station there began the long gruelling walk past all the shops between the station and the seafront. It seemed like a tiresome trudge that would never end, especially with the Mums looking in the shops. Eventually we reached the beach where we would splash about in the mud, build sand castles, eat hard boiled eggs and sandwiches before walking along the pier to spend our pennies in the slot machines at the end. Although there was a train that ran backwards and forwards along the 1.3 miles, we rarely rode on it and if we did it was only on the way back. In the afternoon we visited Peter Pan's Playground enjoying the 'Whip', Helter Skelter, dodgems, big wheel and the crooked house amongst others. After a couple of hours our Mums would drag us back to the Station where we would get the train home.

My Brother, Barry, was born in 1964 and apart from playing with him in the garden and pushing him out to the shops in his pram, it was not a close relationship due to the 13-year age gap. My younger sister, Janine, was born in 1966 and as I left home at the age of 17, I didn't form a close bond with either of them really. However, they are my siblings and will come into the picture later in my story.

Chapter 3 – School Days

I will go back to 1962 when it became time for me to go to secondary school. So, in September 1962 I attended Albany Boys School in Bell Lane, Enfield wearing a shirt and tie, a blazer, short grey trousers and a cap. I remember being terrified due to the rumours that all new boys would be subject to the initiation ceremony of having their heads thrust down the toilets and the flush being pulled. This did, in fact, happen to lots of the new boys but I managed to avoid this embarrassment, I'm not sure how?

Nearly all the boys had long trousers to mark the fact that they had reached the age of 11 and now at big school. I think that I was the last boy in my year to get a pair of long trousers and that wasn't until the end of the first year. It was a tough school and there were some quite undesirable and unpleasant types who attended. Most of those were in the lower stream and as I was in the upper stream avoided any contact with the rougher element for most of the time. Lunchtimes were a hit and miss affair for those who stayed for school dinners, especially for those in their early years there. We had to line up outside the canteen building until the doors opened and we were let in a year at a time with first years getting through the doors last. Once through the door it was a scramble to get to a table that might get you a reasonable chance of a decent portion of food. There would be a teacher at the head of the bench style table and then older students filtering down to the youngest. Food would be collected from the serving hatch in tins and handed along the table to the senior pupils. They would dish out the food and if you had generous servers or the teacher was watching closely you might get a decent portion. The higher up the food chain you were the bigger the portion. Perhaps that's where that expression came from? Another would be the carpet on top of the jugs of custard. These were so named because they had obviously been prepared sometime earlier and left on the counter until ready for collection for pudding. Not only had it formed a skin but also attracted bits of fluff and dust on top, which made it look like a carpet pile. The poor first year at the end of the table was usually the recipient of the carpet.

The discipline was quite strict depending on what teacher you had. Mr Wilmer was the Maths teacher with a frightening reputation. He used to keep a large rubber inner sole inside his brief case and would pull it out slightly at the beginning of the lesson to show he meant business. If you were caught talking when you were supposed to be working he would point at you with his arm outstretched, say, "You boy!" and then turn his hand slowly up the other way and beckon you out to the front of the class where you would receive a hardy whack on the backside from his rubber insole whilst bending over. It definitely had the desired effect as it didn't half sting! If it was your birthday and he found out, he would put your age in chalk back to front on his insole and beckon you to the front of the class to receive your birthday present. This would be a gentler whack on your grey trousered backside where your age the right way round would be shown for the rest of the day. All your class-mates couldn't wait to let Mr. Wilmer know that it was your birthday.

The trip to school was a couple of miles along the Hertford Road and was a fourpenny bus ride. I used to walk to school, however, and meet up with a school mate that lived on the route. I would sometimes walk home thus saving the fourpence, which I would save up for holidays. I remember clearly that the weather was not always clear and in the early 60's we used to get really thick fogs or, 'pea-soupers' where you couldn't see your hand in front of you. On these days we were let out of school early and I would walk home as you couldn't even find the bus stop let alone see a bus coming.

I was never particularly good at sports in general but on sports afternoon on Wednesdays I liked to join the cross-country group. On one long run I managed to tumble down a sharp dip in one of the fields we crossed. After losing my footing I rolled down and cut my leg on a piece of barbed wire that was discarded by someone or had been left there. I still have the scar from that episode. On one occasion prior to leaving for the run, I handed in my watch to one of the games masters, whose name was also Malcolm, to keep it safe. It was a watch left to me by my Grandfather and one that my parents said I should not wear to school. Upon return from the run I asked for my watch and the games master, who had taken us on the run, informed me that the watch had gone missing. There followed an inevitable storm where my parents said, "I told you so." The school put up notices the next day stating that they took no responsibility for any property left on the premises. My parents attended the school and were told that they had investigated with no indication as to who had got access to the games master's room or taken the watch. I avoided speaking to that games master again for the rest of my time at the school. On the day I left he came up to me and said, "You never forgave me for losing that watch, did you?" I said, "No I didn't." and walked away from him. He crops up again later in my story but more about that later.

Each morning we would have a school assembly where we would all file into the main hall and sit cross legged on the floor facing the stage. The Headmaster and all the teachers would be sat on chairs on the stage facing us and a different master would lead the service each day. There would be a reading, a hymn, an address from the Headmaster and always finishing with the Lord's Prayer. When it was the turn of Mr James, the Games master, he always managed to play a pop record for us and justify it somehow as being significant. One day he played, "Good Vibrations" by the Beach Boys, which we all thought was great. The Headmaster always looked stern and I am sure was not happy that we were being played pop music during a religious assembly! As I said already it was a rough school and to avoid the bullies was not always easy. I inevitably became the target one day from a nasty individual, Micky Draper, who decided to humiliate me and make threats if I didn't hand over a ring that I was wearing. I managed to keep hold of the ring pretending that I couldn't get it off my finger but received a thump instead. He also crops up again in my story but more about that later too. Both of these incidents taught me that what goes round comes round is a very true saying.

There were two teachers at the school who had a large influence on me. Mr Allen was the Chemistry and Biology teacher and I always enjoyed his lessons. I ended up being a helper getting things ready for lessons, a sort of Lab assistant. I remember that he took me out on a trip to the pictures to see *How the West was Won* together with his wife.

He also brought me a gift back when he went on holiday. Believe it or not, it was a sheaf knife which I treasured and still have to this day.

The other was Mr Barnes, who was the English teacher. When we first attended lessons, we had ink wells in our desks and pens that you had to put a nib into. It was a task for one of the class to be ink monitor and ensure that before the lesson there was ink in all of the ink wells. When we were eventually allowed to use our own fountain pens, I recall one lad saying, "Sir my pens just run out." Without a beat Mr Barnes said, "Well you'd better run out after it." I get groans from Barbara, my Children and now Grandchildren when I say it after they tell me their pen has just run out. He used to put together and organise a play at Christmas time each year and I joined the group right from the first year. I was a slave of the lamp in *Aladdin*, second Herald in *Robin Hood*, Morgan le fay in *King Arthur*, King Rat in *Dick Whittington*, Amos Culpepper in *Culpepper's Waggon* and Dragon King in *Where the Rainbow Ends*. I always enjoyed these plays each year and it led to my interest in things dramatic and entertaining from then on. I've still got the programmes, photos and press cutting from those plays.

I can't remember how it came about but three of the drama group were asked to perform for a children's party in a local pub. The audience were children from local children's homes. Mick Brooks, who was a close school friend, John Curran and yours truly dressed up as clowns and put on a slapstick routine where we threw custard pies ((paper plates covered with shaving foam) at each other. I have the newspaper clip of that event. Another press clipping from that time reported on a group of members of the Junior Accident Prevention Council (JAPC) giving a talk about safety on the roads to a group of old age pensioners. Yes, you've guessed it, I was a member of that group. As will be shown I am a bit of a hoarder and have all manner of reminders of my past life.

In those days and at that school they seemed to be obsessed with exams and we were annually put through exams in the school hall under strict exam conditions. In the fourth year at Albany we had the Albany Proficiency Certificate where I obtained 4 passes, 5 credits and one distinction in religious education. This was a real surprise as I am not in the least bit religious. The same year I obtained a school certificate in the Royal Society of Arts (RSA) exams. To get the school certificate you had to pass in five subject areas. Mine were Chemistry, English Language, Arithmetic and Mathematics I and II with credit. This was equally surprising to me. In the fifth year was the Certificate in Secondary Education (CSE) where I passed in various grades in 7 subjects. The same year I got 3 passes at 'O' level in the General Certificate in Education (GCE), English Literature, Pure Mathematics and English Language with Spoken English. I'm sure it won't surprise you to know that I still have the certificates and not only that but all the exam papers as well. Sad isn't it!

English Literature wasn't on the school curriculum but for those who wished to take it as a subject, it was offered by Mr James, one of the Games masters, as an after-school option. We were told what to read and study before meeting up round Mr. James's parents' house on Monday nights and Sunday afternoons. There were only four of us as I recall and we used to take our copies of, *Julius Caesar* (Shakespeare) and *The Gun* (C.S. Forester), with us and sit around in his bedroom reading and discussing the books. On a Sunday he would usually still be in his pyjamas and lounging on his bed, with us sitting round in chairs or on the floor. He always had a big plastic keg of cider in his room and we would enjoy a glass whilst having our lesson. It all sounds a bit dodgy now but there was no funny stuff going on, or not that I was witness to anyway. As I mentioned above, I did pass this subject at 'O' level as did all the others, so our time wasn't wasted.

After the Monday evening lesson, I would pop in to visit my Grandma, who lived not far from the bus stop that I caught my bus home. Grandma Trayhorn (My Dad's Mum), lived on her own and was a true character who had led a colourful life. She would insist on cooking me a dinner, which was always meat and two veg. The meat was usually ox tongue. I know! But I always enjoyed it. She had some great stories to tell and liked to talk about her life. She came from a family of eight and due to an accident was unable to walk until she was four. When she was thirteen, her Father rented a barrel organ and they would walk from Ponders End into London where he would play the barrel organ whilst Grandma sang and danced. They became well known in London and the police would apparently hold up traffic so that Grandma could sing and dance. One day they walked to Epsom racecourse where they performed before King Edward VII and Queen Alexandra. As she grew older, she adopted the stage name of Florrie DeVere and had sheet music written for her. She was offered the opportunity to turn professional but as she was under eighteen, she needed her father's permission, which he would not give. She began work in a factory and in 1915 married Edward Trayhorn, my Grandfather. He had been gassed in the great war, was in and out of sanatoriums and died at home aged 39 in 1931. She was left a widow with six children all under the age of fourteen. She had a number of jobs over the years and died in 1977. When I ended my classes on Mondays, I switched to a Friday afternoon and visited every Friday until I left school. I believe that I must have got my entertainment gene from her, a lovely lady.

At the age of 13, I was lucky enough to get a Saturday job at a newsagent in Ordnance Road, Enfield Wash. A mate of mine had been doing this job but wanted to get out of it, so he took me along to the shop and introduced me to the lady who ran the shop. She wasn't keen to let me loose but said she would give me a chance. Most young lads of my age would deliver papers but my job was to go round to people's houses to collect their due fees for paper deliveries. So, with a leather money pouch, a float of cash and a receipt book, I would go round the surrounding streets on my bicycle and knock on the doors. A young face would peer through the window and shout out, "Mum, it's the paper boy." This job was much better than having to get up early every morning to deliver papers and the other benefit was that people saw me in person each week and that led to a far better tip at Christmas. After each round I would go back to the shop, empty out all the money collected and separate the float from the rest. I would use an adding machine, hand operated, to total up the receipt stubs and then see if the total amount on the receipts matched up with the money collected. I was mostly spot on or at least within a few pence. My reward for this round was half a crown (12 ½ pence in new money). Later on, another boy gave up his much longer round and I was offered this for a reward of seven shillings and sixpence. This one I did on Saturday and the shorter round switched to Friday after school.

The shop later moved into the Hertford Road which was a much better spot for passing trade. I became more trusted and ended up looking after the greeting card shelves, keeping them stocked up, tidy and dusted. I was even working behind the counter at times when it was busy. On Friday nights after finishing my duties at the shop I would get on a bus into Waltham Cross and meet up with my Father to do the weekly shop. First it was Palmers, the greengrocers, then Payantakes for some groceries and then Keymarkets for the rest. Saturday afternoons was spent in front of the 'tele' with Dad watching the wrestling and working through the monkey nuts we had got from Palmers the night before. Favourites were Mick McManus, Jackie Pallo, Billy Two Rivers, Giant Haystacks, Catweazel, Big Daddy, Pat Roach and Kendo Nagasaki with commentary by the late and great Kent Walton.

I opened up a post office savings account in 1967 so that I could try and put some of my earnings away. The odd pound here and a few shillings there soon added up. I remember purchasing my first suit from the Co-op store in Enfield Wash for the princely sum of £12. At the rate I was saving and spending I was never going to be a millionaire!

Although Albany was an all-boys school there was an all-girls school right next door and we could see the fairer sex across the quadrangle. So near and yet so far! Girls were not a priority for me whilst I was at school and I didn't really know much about the birds and bees then. It wasn't explained very well during biology lessons apart from the mechanics of what boys had and what girls had. I remember it just led to giggles when pictures of naked people were shown. I certainly never got any guidance from my parents and just had to find things out for myself about love and relationships and protection. All this came later for me.

As I wasn't sure at that time, what I was going to do in the future I made the decision to stay on into the 6th form. This was a momentous time for Albany for it was the year that it changed from a secondary school to a comprehensive. All of a sudden, the two schools became one with boys and girls sitting in the same classrooms together. I became a prefect and by some strange quirk of fate the chairman of the prefects committee. In a sixth form report it was written, "A job he is discharging with real flair." I had to decide when entering the sixth form which subjects to take on for the two-year period of achieving GCE 'A' levels. I opted for English Literature, Advanced Maths and Zoology.

As I came to the end of the first year of my A level courses, it was obvious to me that I was out of my depth. I was finding it difficult to keep up with the progressively hard studies. Maths got more and more complicated and most of it was a mystery to me. English Literature was not really my thing and to this day I am not keen on so called poetry or the strange world of Shakespeare. Zoology was not a taught subject at the school so most of the studies for it were through books and assignments so I was getting nowhere with that.

Mum & Dad

Aged about 18 Months

Nanny Hawkins Southend

Aged about 8

The Holmesdale Gang

On Old London Bridge

Albany Camping Holiday

Me and Barry

Me and Andrew

The Trolley

Cornwall Holiday

1ˢᵗ Car Ford Prefect

Aged about 14

1ˢᵗ Motorbike

Culpepper's Wagon

Dragon King

Chapter 4 – Starting a Career – Cadet Life

I began looking at cutting my losses and finding a future career. I had a hankering for the fire service and at that time they had a cadet programme, which I considered. I also took a keen interest in a career with the Royal Air Force and got all the leaflets with a view to making an application. However, I decided initially to go for a career with the Metropolitan Police and sent off my application to join their cadet scheme. A part of that application required me to attend Cheshunt Police Station to get weighed and measured. Cheshunt Police Station then was in the Metropolitan Police area and just a small building right on the edge of the Old Pond roundabout. Off went my application and back came the reply that at 5'7¼", I was not tall enough and should think about applying when I reached the required 5'8". So, it was back to the drawing board and school life for the time being.

That was until my classmate, Paul told me that he was applying to Hertfordshire Constabulary to join their cadet scheme and why don't I try them? I duly completed the application forms and both he and I were asked to attend the Herts Police HQ at Stanborough, Welwyn Garden City for medical examination and interview. At the end of this process I was informed that although under the minimum height requirement of 5'8" for a Constable, the force medical examiner was of the opinion that I would rise to that dizzy height in the following two years and thus at the joining age, at that time being 19, I would qualify in that respect. There were two very happy chappies who left Herts Police HQ that day to report back that they were to join the cadet corps in September at the age of 17.

It was around this time that I got my first motorbike. It was a Honda 125c.c. for which I paid £60 second hand and was my pride and joy. I clearly remember the registration number as ANK 85B. I still have the invoice and certificate of insurance – told you I was a hoarder!

So it was that in September of 1968 I became a police cadet and moved out of home aged 17 to pursue a career in the police. The two years spent as a cadet were challenging, hard work, physically demanding, educational, stimulating and enjoyable.

As cadets were normally taken on at the age of 16 for a 3-year stint prior to transforming to the exalted rank of Constable, myself and Paul were thrust into the second-year classes. So, I had effectively left home at the age of 17, living in accommodation at Stanborough and adapting to a new life. Life in the cadets back in 1968 was run very much along military lines and challenging to say the least. The days started at 07.15 with a parade on the parade square in PT kit, no matter what the weather. The Drill Sergeant or Duty Officer for the day would then inspect all assembled boys to check that they had shaved and looked in presentable order. Shorts and vests had to be clean and pressed and your plimsolls brilliant white. It depended on who was taking the parade as to what would happen next. The worst-case scenario was that Dickie Cox, the Drill Sergeant, was taking the parade which usually meant a close inspection. "Have you shaved this morning Lad?" "I don't need to shave yet Sergeant." "Well go through the motions Lad, go through the motions." He was full of such rhetoric. Another was, "Are you wearing jewellery Lad?" "It's just my St. Christopher Sergeant." "Take it off this is not a fashion parade." Then after a few warm up exercises, running up and down the parade square, fireman's lifting other cadets or wheelbarrow races, there would follow a cross country run around the surrounding countryside outside HQ. Most of this route is now covered in water and constitutes the Stanborough lakes. On return from the run we would line up again on the parade square only to be told, "Right get your swimming kit and meet in the swimming pool in 5 minutes." When assembled at the end of the pool Dickie would say, "Right 8 lengths breast stroke GO!" Then, "Eight lengths backstroke, GO." Then, "Eight lengths front crawl, GO".

After that we were dismissed to get ready for breakfast. Sometimes we would be pleased to see Inspector Tom Lawrie as the early morning duty officer who would come out to the parade square, say good morning and let us go to get ready for breakfast early and without a lot of running about or swimming. We had breakfast in the canteen at 08.15 when we would have changed into our uniforms. This was a full police style uniform with tunics and bulled up boots. The only difference from a Constable's uniform was the headwear. We had caps with a blue band round the edge denoting a cadet. Shirts in those days were blue cotton with separate collars secured with collar studs. You got 3 collars per shirt so could get away with changing a collar and just ironing the shirt to last for longer before washing. The ties were not clip on ties, that didn't come in until later.

At 08.55 we had to parade again on the parade square in full uniform for inspection. There would be much brushing down of uniforms and checking that there were no hairs or dust showing. Once lined up the Inspecting Officer would walk along the lines of assembled cadets checking that we were all up to standard. Dickie Cox would obviously be most critical, "Look at the dirt in the welt of your boots, you could grow potatoes in them. Are you chewing on parade Lad?" "Yes Sergeant." "Well spit it out, spit it out."

The miscreant, having spat out the offending material onto the parade square would get the response, "That is disgusting, pick it up lad, pick it up." The offender would then have to stand with a gooey and dirty piece of gum in his hand. As he went along behind the rows you would hear, "Am I hurting you lad?" "No Sergeant." "Well I should be because I'm standing on your hair, get it cut, get it cut." After the parade we would go into the classroom to commence a timetable of lessons from 09.00 to 17.00. Subjects covered were, English studies, Economic Geography, Statistics, Principals of Law, Economics and Current Affairs. I was never really sure as to why we studied civil law and not criminal Law, I have never found it useful knowing about the Carlill v the Carbolic Smokeball Company case from 1892. I won't bore you with the details apart from the fact that it revolved around the terms of a contract (Look it up if you are interested!). The lessons would be interspersed with daily periods of P.T., swimming, foot drill and deportment. Evening meal was at 17.30 and then you were free until lights out at 22.30 apart from three cadets who were designated as duty squad. Their duties were to give security patrols around Headquarters and any sundry jobs that the Duty Officer designated. Every Saturday at noon we could go home for the weekend and had to be back by 23.00 on Sunday night. Every fourth weekend we could go home on Friday lunchtime.

Swimming sessions were frequent and taken by a very fit and sporty instructor (nickname *Muddy* as his last name was Waters) who worked you very hard in the pool. We would be swimming up and down the pool doing back stroke, breast stroke, butterfly, side stroke and front crawl. We also spent a lot of time on life saving skills, dragging each other backwards and forwards in the pool. I always struggled to pull someone else through the water and then haul them onto the side of the pool using a technique shown to us. However, I managed to pass the Bronze medallion in life saving. If we worked hard during the session 'Muddy' would split us into two teams for us to play water polo. This was great fun, unless you were in the deep end and had to tread water for long periods of time. Sometimes we would play a water version of British Bulldog. The 'bulldog' would be in the middle of the pool. All remaining players would start off at one end of the pool and swim to the other end of the pool, trying not to be caught by the bulldog. When a player was caught, they become a bulldog themselves. The game continued until all players were caught. On occasions 'Muddy' would join in this game and would give no quarter, if you tried to catch him. Whilst playing this one day I tackled him and we got engaged in a struggle under the water. Unfortunately, I was unable to get out of his grip and ended up struggling for air under water and felt myself losing consciousness. I think he must have sensed that I was in trouble as the next thing I know I was lying on my back on the side of the pool coughing and spluttering with muddy putting me in the recovery position and someone running up with the defibrillator. That was a near death experience I never forgot, although I was to have another of these later in life.

During 1968 there were many things achieved by me, especially in gaining confidence and experiences. Once a week on a Wednesday afternoon and evening a number of us were transported to Sherrard's Training Centre, which was a residence and work premises run by the Spastic's Society. We spent time with the residents working, eating with them and then socialising with them. It wasn't a popular assignment but certainly made you aware of the difficulties that some people experienced and how to communicate with people who were handicapped or had a disability.

The Director of academic studies was known by us as, 'Pea Head', as he was so knowledgeable. I recall that he arranged a trip into London for us to visit museums. There were some cadets who kept him occupied whilst some of us went to Soho and decided to enter an establishment where it advertised live strippers. We paid the entrance fee and walked down a steep set of stairs to a basement area that had a number of rows of cinema style seating facing a small stage. The place was packed and we had to stand at the back. Well I was shocked at the array of ladies coming onto the stage to perform their routines where they ultimately ended up naked of course. When a member of the audience had seen all they wanted, they left leaving an empty seat. Without any polite, "Excuse me", everyone jumped over the seats to get nearer the front. We stayed long enough to get seats in the front rows. The performers did their acts in rotation so we saw the same girls more than once. I think it was the girl that did the performance with a live snake that saw us and said, "Are you lot still here?" It was an interesting day out and I learned a lot!

Once a week we would attend Welwyn Garden City college where we used to go for lessons in technology and design. We had to march the 1 mile from HQ to the college and were supposed to march back. The local residents and visitors to the town must have marvelled at the sight of lines of police cadets in full uniform marching along the streets. Sometimes we took taxis to get back to HQ to ensure we were in the canteen queue in time for lunch. That was fine until one stupid driver took one load right up the training block doors and in front of the Drill Sergeant.

Once a year there was a two-week training course away from HQ at Pendley Manor near Tring. This was a historic mansion dating back to 1872. The owner at the time we visited in September 1968, was BBC show jumping commentator Dorian Williams. There was a structured timetable with parades and inspections in the driveway outside the Mansion and a number of guest speakers on a variety of subjects. It was truly a wonderful two weeks and hard to think how much effort went into its organisation.

As I think I have already mentioned, I was not a great sportsman and although I participated in sporting activities and was very fit, I was not good enough for the football, cricket, rugby or any team games really. Come the selection of cadets to represent their class at the annual sports day in June of 1968 all the best runners, hurdlers, high jumpers, discus and javelin throwers were selected leaving yours truly standing like the last unwanted coffee cream in a selection box. The PTI making the selections said, "You're bloody useless Trayhorn, there's nobody doing the mile walk so you can do that."

So, whilst everyone was throwing javelins, shot putting and sprinting I just walked round the football pitch. On sports day, much to my surprise, I found myself out in front and literally 'walked it', coming first. What a great feeling it was that I had been good at something and achieved a win at a sports related event. I still have my small Wedgewood vase as the prize for winning.

In April 1969 I was chosen as one of eight to represent Hertfordshire in the National Association of Boy's Clubs Annual National Inter-County Cross Country Championship in Sutton Coldfield. I can't remember what position I finished but seem to remember I didn't do bad and as I had represented Hertfordshire qualified for my county colours, which obviously I still have!

I was subsequently chosen to represent Hertfordshire in the Cadet's National Inter Force Athletic Competition Cup on Saturday 21st June 1969 at the Gosling stadium, Welwyn Garden City. There were 12 competitors for the mile walk from all round the country and the previous record for the event was held by someone from Birmingham at 8min.26.1 secs. the previous year. I remember the race as if it were yesterday and in the early stages of the race I was in the running, or should I say walking! Entering the last lap there were two others in front of me but I was determined to catch them so went into my best heel-toe technique being careful not to break out into a run. In the final straight I managed to get in front with great cheers from spectators and crossed the line in first place. Not only that but I had broken the standing record with a time of 7min. 52.6 secs. I had my picture taken crossing the finishing line and it appeared in the local paper. I have that cutting in my collection.

Another annual event was an outward-bound course to Snowdonia led by Dickie Cox and staff Colantine. We stayed in an old building halfway up a mountain track which was pretty sparse and the sleeping accommodation was a dormitory style room on the first floor. Cooking was done on primus stoves outside and the washing facility was the stream running past nearby. There was the daily inspection by Dickie Cox when he would check that the beds were made up and blankets folded to exact instructions and laid out on top of the bed together with shining aluminium billy cans, cutlery and washing gear. As Dickie walked along, he would pick up an item say it wasn't up to standard and throw it out of the window. At the end of inspection, you had to retrieve your item from a stack on the ground outside the window.

We went on numerous expeditions, mostly in the rain and carrying heavy packs. One expedition was to the top of Snowdon. So, I had achieved reaching the top of one of the three peaks (only two more to go!). On one outing we stopped for a well-earned break at a large boulder which was known as Gladstone Rock.

Apparently on 13th sept 1892 the right honourable W. E. Gladstone M.P. when prime minster for the fourth time and 83 years old, addressed the people of Eryri from this rock, upon justice to Wales. I don't know what prompted me but I got up on top of the rock and gave a speech to the bedraggled and exhausted group before me. I have no recollection of what I spoke about, it was probably a complete load of rubbish (as was Gladstone's probably?) I attended a cadet reunion a couple of years ago and was speaking to a member of that group about our outward-bound expedition in Wales. He said that my giving a speech from the rock was one of the things he remembers most about that trip. Perhaps I should have run for member of parliament!

When we got back from one trip, Dickie decided that we should have a game of football. "But Sergeant, there isn't a football field anywhere near here?" We followed him a short distance up the track to a small flat piece of ground that had previously been occupied by cattle, as could be determined by there being cow pats covering most of it. So, we played football halfway up a mountain rolling about in cow shit – nice!

One walk we went on was actually in good weather and we were sweating in all our gear and came out eventually next to a road where the support van was waiting. Out of the back was produced a supply of ice-cold cans of shandy. I cannot remember any drink tasting so sweet and being so satisfying. At that time, it was the highlight of my life and probably reminiscent of that moment in the film, 'Ice Cold in Alex,' when John Mills, Sylvia Sims and Anthony Quayle each have a glass of beer with beads of moisture running down the side of the glass.

We were paid a nominal wage at the end of each month and for the month of October 1968 the grand sum of twenty-two pounds five shillings and two pence was presented to me.

In February 1969 I was delegated to attend with Peter, another cadet, the Sea Salter holiday park near Whitstable in Kent. This was a camp run by the Shaftesbury Society for disabled people and their families. So, in August myself and Peter joined families for a week's holiday. Peter and I pitched in with all activities and because we were having a great time then so were the families.

The transport was an old Bedford Dormobile with a stick shift gear lever and Peter and I were allowed to drive it around the field within the grounds. It was probably where I first learned the art of driving and clutch control. The week was a real hoot with us interacting with the disabled, joining in the fun and activities. I have great pictures of Peter and myself wearing straw hats and with stupid grins on our faces as well as me made up as Frankenstein's monster for the fancy dress competition. Peter and I did get the opportunity to visit a local pub and it was where I first experienced the game of shove halfpenny and bar skittles. I learnt a lot during that week about working with disabled individuals and their families. We both got a lot of thanks and compliments from the people that we had spent the week with.

Chapter 5 – Senior Cadet Life

After a year I was elevated to the dizzy height of being a "Senior Cadet". This meant that we were attached to a police station near to our home and would observe, under guidance from experienced officers, what goes on in the real world of policing. There were also certain experiential attachments and regular attendances back to Headquarters to ensure standards were being observed. Paul, my old school chum and I were both posted to Hoddesdon Police Station. It was whilst out on patrol with a Constable I was involved in an arrest, my first even though I wasn't the arresting officer. We had been called to a house on the edge of town where certain items had gone missing from a washing line. The culprit was caught nearby with his ill-gotten gains. He was dubbed the Knicker Knocker of Old Hoddesdon Town.

In November of 1969 I was to attend a month-long outward-bound course at the outward-bound mountain school in Eskdale, Cumbria. This was attended by young 17/18-year olds from all different walks of life and from all parts of the country. Being in November and December it was freezing cold and there was a lot of snow and ice in the mountains. We were taught mountaineering skills and survival techniques plus team work. In the mornings we would have to run down from our minimal, bunk bed, accommodation to a shower block where we had to strip off and stand under a shower to await the water being turned on. You could hear a cacophony of screams as the freezing cold water cascaded down and you applied soap as quickly as you could so that the torture would stop.

I was a member of a team of ten and we had the name of Nansen patrol. There were many activities during the month including: – Abseiling, rock climbing, an outdoor circuit training course, a tree-top rope course, a parachute style jump from a tall tree, a stretcher carrying exercise, map and compass reading, tent pitching (blindfolded), cooking on a primus stove, a steeplechase, overnight camping, zip wire, knot tying, orienteering, volley ball and expeditions up hills and mountains.

One expedition was to the top of Scafell Pike, the highest peak in England. (So, two down just one to go!) I can't really say that the scenery was spectacular as it was mostly snow and ice everywhere you looked, with poor visibility. We carried back packs and an ice pick, which we were shown how to use should we lose our footing and slip down the treacherous slopes. This we had to practice on a safer but still steep, slope. You had to stand with your back to the slope and then fall backwards sliding down the slope rapidly. The trick was to stick the pointed end of the ice pick into the snow, spin round and put your full weight on it so as to slow your descent and bring you to a stop. It was tough, with not all those who started out, completing the course, but I received my certificate in the end for successful completion.

An interesting, eye opening and embarrassing attachment was the two weeks spent at Hertford County Hospital. One week in casualty and one week on the wards. Although wearing my uniform, apart from tunic and cap, I wore a doctor's white coat, so as far as members of the public were concerned, I was just a member of hospital staff. There were a variety of casualties coming into the casualty department from heart attacks to minor cuts. I mostly observed or pushed wheelchairs and trolleys about plus running backwards and forwards to the X-Ray department.

The week on the geriatric ward was less exciting and revolved around emptying bottles and bedpans and helping to clean up patients too frail to go to the toilet. Not a job I saw myself doing full time and the nursing profession will always be right up there among my heroes. The Sister in charge of the ward asked me if I would take on the role of shaving the elderly men who were unable to shave themselves, as she liked her male patients to look clean and free of unwanted facial hair. I got to work each morning with a supply of shaving soap, brush and razors doing the rounds of patients requiring a shave. One morning the Sister said that the Orderly that did the shaves on another ward had gone sick and asked me if I would do the shaves on that ward. Of course, I was happy to oblige and turned up with the equipment to be told that the man requiring a shave was in a bed behind screens in the corner. I duly lathered up my brush and applied the lather around his face in preparation. The Sister poked her head round the corner of the screen and with a large grin on her face said, "No not there, he is having an appendix operation and needs to be shaved from his stomach down to his knees". If I could have escaped or have the ground open up, I would have found it a great relief from my embarrassment or to get me out of having to perform this task. As I couldn't, I just had to get on with it. I applied copious amounts of lather around his nether regions, as I had no knowledge of how to shave this area of a male anatomy. I certainly didn't shave that area on myself! In order to shave the scrotal area, I had to grab hold of a very limp appendage, lift it up with one hand and apply the razor with the other. The patient tried to make conversation and was telling me how he had been the Vicar in Wolverhampton and knew Enoch Powell. He then said, "You're very young to be a Ward Orderly." I said, "Well actually I'm not, I'm just a Police Cadet in training." Well his face was a picture, sort of amazement coupled with a hint of panic. However, I finished the job and managed to successfully complete my two weeks attachment.

Another Attachment was to a Scenes of Crime Officer in late 1969. In those days this job was always performed by a Detective Sergeant and I tagged along with him to scenes of crime. Terry was a very nice man who drove a VW Beetle. I remember going to a large country house where they had been burgled and after looking at the point of entry and flicking fingerprint dust around the relevant areas, we were offered a cup of tea. The cup and saucer that was presented was huge and tea poured from a fancy tea pot. The liquid that appeared in the cup did not resemble any tea that I had ever seen, it smelt like coal dust and probably tasted like it. It was absolutely disgusting and I don't know how I managed to get it down, or keep it down for that matter! The timing of this attachment proved to be perfect for me as this was the time of a high-profile murder enquiry.

A Mrs Muriel McKay, who was the wife of Rupert Murdoch's Deputy, had been kidnapped on the evening of 29th December 1969. The kidnappers had followed the Murdoch's company Rolls Royce to Mrs McKay's home after mistakenly thinking that it was Anna Murdoch. The car had been lent to them whilst the Murdoch's were in Australia. Her husband reported her missing at 8.00 pm, after he returned home and found the telephone ripped from the wall and the content of his wife's handbag scattered on the stairs. The kidnappers were eventually traced to Rooks farm near Stocking Pelham and suspected to be the Hussein Brothers. It was strongly suspected that they had killed Mrs. McKay and buried her body somewhere on the farm. Terry's job was to examine any bones that were discovered during the search of the surrounding area. We did look at a number of bones mostly discovered by dogs but they all turned out to be non-human. Her body was in fact, never discovered and it was the first case in many years where suspects were convicted of murder with no body being found.

There was also the Traffic attachment where I got to ride around in the back of a Mk II Jaguar on the A1M motorway and also in the first Range Rover possessed by Herts Constabulary. One call was to a lorry drivers assistant who had fallen out of the cab on the motorway whilst leaning out to check the load (He survived). Speed traps were a bit different then and required a lot of heavy equipment. A big box containing the radar was placed at the side of the road, a wire attached to that ran along the side for a distance of around 150yds where there would be a speed meter. If someone was clocked above the limit a race would ensue to get the vehicle stopped before it got too far. Apart from gaining experience in dealing with accidents and traffic control I wasn't excited about traffic policing and so wouldn't be looking to go down that road!

CID attachment also, was not an experience that gave me any aspirations to become a detective. For one thing, they were a fairly close-knit bunch and although worked well with the uniform officers they tended to keep most things to themselves and certainly were not going to trust a spotty faced inexperienced cadet. I was relegated mostly to filing pieces of paper in the CID office and not until the second week, did I get out and about with a detective. I can't tell you some of the things I experienced but I did learn that a part of the role of a good detective was to drink. This got you good contacts and information about what was happening locally in the villain's world. The expression, 'It takes a thief to catch a thief,' springs to mind. On one outing we recovered a large number of films from a suspect's premises and set up a projector in the CID office to check the contents. This was my first experience of pornography and opened my eyes as much as some of the porn stars were opening their legs. I never suspected that there was so much depravity and depths that people would stoop to. Modesty forbids me to describe in any detail some of the scenes.

Hertfordshire Constabulary had a scheme that if you were a senior cadet without a driving licence, they would give you a driving course and teach you the police system of driving early. Then they would put you through a test so that when you returned from your Constable training course you would immediately be of a standard and not have to go on a further conversion course. I mention this because whilst on the course I learned a valuable lesson and it wasn't to do with driving. We were out on an instructional drive one day when the instructor had a call via the in-car radio to return to Headquarters. It turned out that there had been a murder at Garston, near Watford and it was the responsibility of the HQ traffic officers to take the mobile police station to the scene and set it up ready for use by investigating officers. Myself and the other cadet went with the driver to help set up the caravan.

We got to the scene and began to set things up and I was asked to keep people back whilst everything was got ready. There were one or two people who said they had witnessed something prior to the body of a young woman having been found in a nearby wood. I stood talking to them and one chap in particular who had a bike with him and was telling me about someone he had seen lurking about. It turned out some time later that this chap was in fact the perpetrator of a particularly brutal rape and murder. So, the lesson was that you don't trust anything anyone tells you and don't take things at face value. I later learnt that when a suspect is being questioned and they say, "No it wasn't me officer on my life," it means they are probably lying. If they say," On my Baby's life," it means they are definitely lying!!

When I passed my driving test, I bought myself my first car It was a 1952 Ford Prefect for which I paid £40, a good price due to the fact that there was no driver's side window. The registration number was RMY 175 and yes, I still have the receipt for it as well as a picture (unfortunately not the car though). You could work on cars then as there was easy access to the small engine under the large bonnet. It had rod and cable brakes and a transverse suspension. The windscreen could open up from the bottom by using a large wing nut. If the battery went flat, which was a regular occurrence, you just got out the starting handle turned it over and the engine would spark into life. The missing window was not a problem as you could just take a few tools with you to the local scrapyard, clamber about amongst the old wrecks piled up until you came across a scrapped car the same model as yours. You would then take what you wanted and give the man at the gate a few shillings.

It was in this car that I got my first parking ticket. I was required to spend some time at "A" Division headquarters, Hertford Police station which was then in Castle Street. I parked in the square in the middle of the town and was blissfully unaware as I sat in the warrant office at the station that there was a time restriction applying and I subsequently returned to my car to find a parking ticket attached. I paid the £2 fine and kept it very quiet. I still have that ticket receipt as well as one other for £6 some years later.

On 19th July 1969 together with all the cadets ending their time as a cadet, I paraded back at Stanborough for a final inspection and presentation of awards by Lieutenant Colonel L.R.H.G Leach, M.C., D.L.

Chapter 6 – Transforming into a Constable

In the first week of August 1970 I travelled to Eynsham Hall in Witney, Oxfordshire to start my 13-week training programme to qualify as a full Constable. I had to return to HQ on 13th August to be attested as I was not 19 when I started at Eynsham. I suppose I must have been the youngest PC at that time having been attested on my 19th Birthday. At that time forces would send their trainee Constables to District Training Schools, so apart from Hertfordshire Constabulary there were guys from Bedfordshire and Luton, Thames Valley, Essex, City of London and Suffolk on my course. Eynsham Hall was an old country mansion dating back to 1906. It was used by various people until 1946 when it was taken over by the Home Office for use as a training school. Nowadays it is a Hotel and conference centre. The living accommodation was dormitories with shared wash room facilities and communal dining room, which was strictly formal. The regime at the school was fairly strict but our class instructor was a very mild mannered and thoroughly nice Sergeant. Learning of the law was given from a text book called, *Moriarty's Police Law* and covered every subject you could think of. There were three exams to pass during the course, junior, intermediate and senior. Guess what, I still have those exam papers, and my copy of Moriarty's Police Law! On Wednesday afternoons there was a choice of football or cross country for Games afternoon. You'll never guess which one I chose? One of the advantages was that once you had finished the 5-mile run you could get your bath (there were no showers) in and get on with your studies before the football crowd had to fight over the minimal bathing facilities. Towards the end of each course there was a Chief Constable's Challenge Shield awarded by the reviewing officer at the passing out parade, for the winner of the course five-mile cross country run. I am proud to brag that I won the race and was presented with the shield at the passing-out parade on 6th November 1970. This is in pride of place amongst my other memorabilia.

I made some good friends whilst at Eynsham but one that I especially had an affinity with was Neil, who was with Suffolk Constabulary. I kept in touch with him after we left the training school and spent a short break with him at his mother's house in Southwold. Walking along the seafront with his dog was a memorable experience and gave me a long-time fondness for Southwold. We had planned to go on a trip together to Europe but before it happened, I met and was courting my future wife.

Some years later and on my recommendation, he transferred to the Metropolitan Police but we then lost contact. I am glad to say that whilst researching and writing this book I received a message from Neil. He had tracked me down through social media after over 50 years and we are now back in contact.

Chapter 7 – My First Station as Constable

It was in October of 1970 that I was given my first posting as a Constable and much to my surprise I was sent back to Hoddesdon. I believe that this was because I could stay at my parent's house five miles down the road and not because I had been requested. This was short lived, however because a brief time later a new police station was opened up in Hertford which had a single officers' accommodation hostel built at the side. A room of my own with a bed, wardrobe and wash basin – luxury. The toilets and showers were communal however, together with a communal kitchen.

As there were no carpets on the floor, myself and a couple of the lads approached a carpet shop on our patch and asked them if they had any spare sample squares we could have. We managed to secure enough to make patchwork carpeting in several rooms in the hostel with the use of double-sided carpet tape. During my time there I made some life-long friends and had some great times, more of which later.

I duly attended Hoddesdon Nick for my first tour of duty and found a much more relaxed atmosphere. The first thing to do on an early turn shift (06.00 to 14.00) was to make the tea and have a briefing from the Sergeant. Although in the 70's, I look back now and make comparisons with what I see when watching an episode of Heartbeat. Apart from it being a small town and not a rural setting, the policing style had a lot of similarities. I was taken out in a panda with a PC who had 9 years' experience. One of the first things he said to me was, "Forget all that rubbish they told you at training school, you just nick 'em, stick 'em and make sure they go down at court." He was joking, of course but there was definitely a sort of code between cops and villains.

One of my first reports was in relation to an accident I witnessed on 11th November 1970. I was acting as a prisoner escort for two prisoners that were to be delivered to Pentonville and Brixton Prisons. The Divisional transport, a Bedford Dormobile, was being driven by a civilian with myself and two other constables in the back handcuffed to the prisoners. We reached Pentonville prison first and were parked in the yard just inside the front security gates. One prisoner was being taken inside whilst I remained in the Dormobile with the other PC and prisoner to be taken to Brixton. I noticed a large coach enter the yard and start to reverse towards where we were parked. I could see that he wasn't going to stop so shouted out as I couldn't get out due to being handcuffed to the prisoner. The front of the Dormobile was damaged but as I recall we still delivered the other prisoner to Brixton. This type of prisoner escort was a fairly regular occurrence at that time, although the accidents were not.

Although most of the time was spent attending incidents and patrolling in cars, there were plenty of times you were expected to patrol the High Street on foot. This was especially so on night duty (22.00 – 06.00) when you had to check every property in the High Street, front and back, a practise referred to as, "shaking door handles." Woe betide you if a break-in was found at any of these premises the following day. If there was, you would be dragged out of bed to appear in front of the Chief Inspector and explain why you had not found it. This happened to Fred, a colleague and life-long friend of mine.

I couldn't help looking at my reflection in the shop windows as I walked along. Could that smart looking policeman really be me? At one end of the High Street was a petrol station from where you could stand and glare menacingly at the lorries speeding along the road from the Sainsbury's depot just before the end of night duty. Whilst standing there one day a colleague pulled up in his panda car and I bent down, taking off my helmet, to speak to him. When he drove off, I stood back up, put my helmet back on and resumed my menacing looks towards the lorry drivers. It didn't seem to be having much effect because they all seemed to be laughing at me. It wasn't until I was halfway back to the Station that I realised that I had put my helmet on back-to-front!

I can't remember the order of things happening over the next four years but will recall things I remember clearly. There was a baker at the end of the High Street that used to bake bread and doughnuts early in the morning and we would pop in there to get warm and get a bag of doughnuts. I was out driving with the Sergeant early one morning when we were greeted by the sight of my mate Steve struggling along a back street towards the nick with a bag full of doughnuts, which he foolishly tried to hide under his coat. His punishment was to share the hoard with everyone at the nick over a cup of tea, which he had to make.

One thing I found during my early days as a young bobby was that I had frequent comments about my youthful looks. If I heard, "You're very young for a Policeman," once, I heard it a hundred times. The other one was, "I must be getting old as the coppers are looking younger." In order to try looking older, I decided to grow a moustache. Although it took some time and was a bit scrawny looking, I persevered and kept it for over 25 years.

In the Town centre there was a block of high-rise flats with a number of shops at ground level and in the corner next to Woolworths was a bowling alley. This was an eerie place to walk round at night and it was a sort of initiation for new Constables to be given the duty of checking the properties at night. Whilst he was creeping round in the dead of night with not a sound, a couple of longer serving chaps would be looking down from one of the balconies of the block of flats high above. At the right moment a fluorescent light tube would be dropped and would explode upon impact. The young newby would be shitting himself whilst everyone else was in fits of laughter. It must have woken up a few of the flats residents as well – what a bunch of hooligans!

One night we were conducting stops in the High Street to see who was passing through and checking for irregularities or drink drivers. We had one car stopped and my colleague was speaking to the driver when I heard the roar of a car engine descending on us. I stepped forward and shone my torch in the direction of the fast-approaching vehicle and raised my hand in a command for the driver to stop. He obviously did not see me in time as at the last moment went into a skid and slid for a long distance ending up embedded in the back of the car we had previously stopped. I can't remember how we got out of that one, but we did!

Friday night would sometimes get quite rowdy in the Town, with groups of youths causing trouble and making a nuisance of themselves. We would have a rowdyism patrol from 22.00 to midnight, in order to counter this problem. Officers on late shift would stay on for an extra two hours to bolster numbers. One night we got a call to the Rye House Tavern, a popular drinking establishment right next to the river, where a group of youths were reported to be causing trouble. I was accompanied by a Sergeant and drove the panda to the scene, meeting others at the premises. Upon arrival the publican said that the offending youths had fled the scene but had released their collection of canoes and they had drifted off down the river. After a quick search of the area it was obvious that there was nobody to apprehend so our attention focussed on helping to retrieve the canoes which had come to a rest a bit further along the river close to the opposite bank. Unfortunately, they were just out of reach so the Sergeant and I went in search of a boat hook from a nearby boat yard. We found one but as it was twice the length of the panda the Sergeant had to hold onto it out of the passenger window while I drove the car along to the appropriate spot.

It was a bit like medieval jousting only with a car instead of a horse! We thankfully managed to hook in the canoes and each of us took one and paddled it back over to the pub to much amusement and laughter. Upon getting out one officer had to get across from one boat to another and ended up doing a precarious version of the splits over the water. As he tried to gain his composure the personal radio that was clipped inside his tunic fell out and disappeared into the river. Being dark we couldn't locate it so a large torch was obtained from a lorry driver nearby, which we placed in a large plastic bag to prevent it from getting wet. I took off my tunic and rolled up my sleeve so that I could lean over the side of a canoe, immerse the torch under the water and try to locate the now soggy radio. The Sergeant stood on the bank with the boat hook pulling the reeds apart until we spied the expensive piece of equipment. Now located, the officer who had dropped it stripped off to his underpants and dived in to the depths (about 3 feet) to retrieve it. We all returned to the station, some of us soggy and one semi-naked, all in fits of laughter to be greeted by a visiting Chief Inspector. He took one look at us and said, "I won't ask, I'll be at Bishops Stortford if you need me." The radio was put on the radiator to dry off but I don't think it ever worked again, we all said it was a mystery and must be a piece of faulty equipment.

Visiting senior officers were quite common and they always liked to find something wrong. One Superintendent was particularly meticulous at checking the books, especially the General Occurrence Book (G.O.B.) The instructions were that at midnight the Station Duty Officer (S.D.O.) usually a trusted long serving Constable, had to write in the date in red ink and underline it. The Superintendent's first name was Bernard but everyone referred to him as, "Bernie-the-bolt!" In order to stop him finding something more serious to moan about or find wrong, the date would remain without being underlined. Once he had admonished the S.D.O. for this heinous omission he would happily make his way to somewhere else. Obviously, the next station would be forewarned of his impending arrival so they could prepare some minor discrepancy for him to find.

I remember that Steve and myself were out in a panda one night visiting the Rye House Go-cart track, which at the dead of night was perfect for time trials of the panda car on the circuit. Over the radio came the call, "Alpha 29, what is your location for a rendezvous?" The voice was obviously that of Bernie and we couldn't possibly reveal that we were somewhere we shouldn't have been so we told him that we were at Broxbourne railway station. "I will meet you there in 10 minutes." We sped our way to the Rail Station hoping that we didn't go flying past the Superintendent in his car. Once there it was a panic to make some entries in the patrol diary, which we had not completed, as required, that night. When Bernie arrived, he got out and spoke to Steve, who was the designated driver. He asked to see the patrol log and appeared satisfied so we thought we had got away with it. However, he said, "I think I'll have a look at your pocket book lad." Steve handed over his pocket book and upon examination said, "This pocket book is two days out of date." "Sorry sir I still have some entries to make yet." Replied Steve. Bernie then proceeded to give him a lecture about original notes and the need to keep books up-to-date. He then turned to me and said, "I think I'll have a look at your pocket book too Lad." Of course, mine was likewise out-of-date. "Right I'll see both of you in my office at 9 o'clock tomorrow morning, your pocket books better be up-to-date and you can expect fireworks." So, we had little or no sleep after finishing at 06.00 and then having to make up our pocket books and appear in front of Bernie at 09.00.

One of the signs of a good copper was getting to know the patch, knowing the villains, the yobs and most importantly those places that were pro-police and you could be assured of a cup of tea or refreshments. One of my tea stops was at the back of a dry-cleaning shop where you got a decent cuppa and as a bonus chat with the lovely young lady who worked there. Everyone had their preferred tea stops. I sometimes frequented the rear of the Beefeater restaurant where you might get a steak sandwich if the owner was around. I was in the kitchen one night, chatting with the owner's wife when her husband came in. He greeted me warmly and asked if I'd had my steak sandwich. When he discovered that I had not, he gave his wife a firm ticking off with some choice Greek language and instructed her to get me something to eat. I was already embarrassed by this point especially at the thought that I had possibly been the initiator of a domestic incident, something which I seemed to spend a lot of my time trying to arbitrate never mind instigate. I was even further embarrassed when, a short time later, a full steak dinner with all the trimmings was put in front of me. For the sake of good police/public relations I forced it down!

Another good place was the security gate at a National store's warehouse, where you could get a full dinner during the night shift at a very good price. I would ring the guys on the gate and order a meal, telling them what time I would be there. When I turned up, one of the guards would walk over to the canteen and bring back a tray with the meal which I would eat in the gatehouse.

There was also a signal box where you could get a cuppa and a warm by a really good fire and the rear door of the George pub where I had an arrangement on a Sunday to pop in for what was left after Sunday lunches. This was endearingly referred to as, "the scrapings." One Sunday, whilst I was at a briefing with the Sergeant and the whole shift, the Station Duty Officer (S.D.O.) came in and announced, "The landlady at the George wants to know if you are calling in for your scrapings?" My colleagues burst out laughing and the Sergeant gave me a dirty look and a ticking off.

I don't want to give the impression that it was all mucking about and fun, there were also some quite traumatic and difficult assignments. Early one icy, misty morning I was driving along a road leading through the country part of my patrol area when I came across a car which had come off the road and was embedded in a tree. There was a windscreen lying in the middle of the road and as I approached, I could see the driver slumped forward over the steering wheel and could hear a horrible gasping breathing sound. I pulled the man back to assess his injuries and found that there was a lot of blood plus one of his eyes had been pulled out it's socket and was hanging down his face. It appeared that upon impact the windscreen had been knocked out as he was thrown forward and the windscreen wiper had twisted round and had pierced his eye socket. Worse than that was the white matter splattered over the roof interior which I guessed was brain matter. I called for an ambulance on my radio and dashed back to the panda to get the first aid kit. Unfortunately, it was missing so I was very pleased when the ambulance turned up. As it happened there was very little that I nor anyone else could do to save this unfortunate man, although he did survive until the next day. It taught me to check that the first aid box is in the panda at the start of every shift! Mind you I doubt that a few plasters, bandages or arm slings would have been much use.

Although a single chap at that time I liked to get involved in the social side of things and during my time at Hoddesdon held the positions of bar manager and social secretary, although not at the same time! The top floor of the nick had a canteen, a bar and a large area for holding social events. When there was a social event, during the interval, a couple of the lads and myself would lay on a bit of entertainment. My contribution was to take off the Singing Postman and Tommy Cooper as well as a few of us performing a rendition of, 'A Policeman's lot is not a happy one', from The Pirates of Penzance by Gilbert and Sullivan. For the Tommy Cooper routine, I had gathered a small collection of hats and made up a stupid poem incorporating them. It went down well and I have been asked to perform it countless times over the years since, although I have had to change it every time I lose a hat and add a new one. I had made a Fez out of cardboard, which was not very good but a local resident, who was at one of the functions, I think his wife was the Mayor at the time, said, "You need a proper Fez I have one for you which comes from Morocco" This is the one I have used ever since.

For one of the social nights I organised, with the local fish & chip shop, that they would provide us with a large order of fish & chips or chicken & chips as the refreshments during the interval. This was agreed as long as I collected them from the shop. As the time approached for the interval I jumped into my car and sped to the chippie. He had half the order ready so I took that back to the station placed it in the service lift to the kitchen and climbed the stairs to retrieve them at the top. I wanted to serve all portions at the same time so lit the gas ovens in the kitchen, shoved the 40-50 portions inside to keep warm whilst I collected the second batch. Back I went, collected the remaining part of the order and back to the station. Up the stairs after putting the order in the service lift and when I got to the top I was greeted by panic. People running round with fire extinguishers and smoke billowing out of the kitchen and the oven. I spent ages trying to retrieve what I could from the resulting charred remains and share out the unspoilt portions. Needless to say, I was not responsible for the refreshments at the next bash!

Noisy parties were a regular call on late shifts with an irate individual ringing up to complain about noise emanating from a neighbour's house. Most times a visit and quiet word at the offending property would do the trick. I called at one house and when the door was opened, I was faced with people all dressed in roaring twenties outfits. I told them that a neighbour had complained and they said that they were surprised as most neighbours were actually at the party. It was a farewell bash as they were moving later that week. I told them to enjoy the party, to wait until I was round the corner and then turn the music back up. "Come in for a drink officer." "No thanks not whilst on duty but good luck with the move and enjoy the rest of the night." I returned to the station as it was close to booking off time. I told my mate Steve about the party and said I might call in on the way home to see if it was still going on. I did just that and the party was still in full swing. I knocked on the door and when opened the lady said, "Oh no not another complaint." I said, "No I just thought I would take you up on your offer of a drink now that I am off duty." I was welcomed in and introduced to the crowd inside as a loud cheer went up at the late arrival. I had a beer thrust into my hand and was told to help myself to the magnificent spread that was set out in the kitchen. After about 30 minutes, whilst I was in the kitchen, drinking, stuffing my face and chatting, there was another loud cheer closely followed by Steve entering the kitchen to join me. We had a great night drinking, eating and dancing until about two in the morning when most of the attendees started to flag.

Steve and I decided to say thank you to our hosts by performing our comedy routine. This took the form of jokes from Steve and then a Tommy Cooper routine from me. I had my box full of hats that I used in the boot of the car so on we went with our little show. All the party goers sat round in the living room whilst we drunkenly put on a show. We got a rapturous applause at the end and one of the audience came up to us afterwards and said that he was an organiser at the local British Legion Club and would we come and do our routine there on a Saturday night. We actually did do just that and were told that we were welcome back any time.

After night duty we would get into my car, now a Hillman Minx registration RNJ 118 bought for £30 from another PC at the station, or Steve's Mk II Ford Cortina hand painted bright yellow with a green stripe down each side. We would drive to Frinton, Walton-on-the-Naze or Clacton, stopping at a greasy spoon café on the way for a fry-up breakfast. Once there we would sleep on the beach and only head back so that we had time to get changed into uniform ready for the next nights duty. If it was early turn, Steve and I would drive round in a panda until we found a milkman. We would purchase a pint of gold top each and share a packet of chocolate digestives whilst parked up somewhere out of the way.

Steve was another occupant of the single men's hostel at the side of what was then the brand-new police station in Ware Road, Hertford. Other close chums at that time were Dave, Fred and Colin. Colin Fred and I would spend a lot of time together, mostly drinking and playing cards. Three card brag was our game of choice and we would play for the odd change we had saved up. We regularly used to frequent the Saracen's Head pub just down the road and spend money on beer and the fruit machine. The landlord was Big Ron and we regularly won money on his machine. I'm sure his settings were not calibrated in his favour but any winnings were ploughed back into his coffers. We would order steak & kidney pies and baked beans which he would cook in the wonder that was a micro-wave oven (Quite revolutionary then).

Another place we spent a lot of time was the "Hole in the Wall club." This was a small bar located at the towns retained fire station, which also doubled up as an ambulance depot. If we were on early turn after our 06.00 tea and briefing at the station, we would be at the Ambulance office by 07.00 for the start of their tour and tea time. Getting back to the Hole in the Wall club, we would usually be there in the evening when not on duty, after 23.00 as the person who opened the bar would not have rolled out of the local pub until then. Cyril was the person who opened up and he was a retained fireman as well as running his own local engineering business. The three of us, but especially Fred and I, would spend hours drinking and putting the world to rights. Another visitor to the club was a local bookmaker who had his own betting shop, I believe his name was Reggie Banks. A party piece I had was to drink a pint of beer in one go whilst standing on my head. We were talking about this one night and Reggie said it couldn't be done, so money was put on it and I was soon on my head, Fred holding my legs whilst a pint glass of beer was placed on the floor in front of my face. I duly consumed the pint and so won the bet.

Cyril would sometimes say that he was going home as it was late and he had had enough drink so he would leave us the keys and tell us to lock up behind us. We had a good relationship with the retained firemen and the ambulance crew. We had a call to an ice cream van that had caught fire down towards Rye House sewage works and when we arrived on scene the van was well alight and the fire brigade had two hoses trained on it. As we approached the mischievous guys holding one of the hoses allowed the nozzle to point in our direction, drenching us. We promptly grabbed the other hose to return the compliment and ended up having a water fight with the ice cream van fast disappearing and the Italian van owner leaping up and down. To be fair the van was a gonner anyway!

Talking about ice-cream vans reminds me of another encounter I had that indirectly related to one. I was on duty driving my panda one day when my attention was drawn to a speeding car. I followed it for a short distance before pulling the driver over. It turned out to be a very apologetic Italian man. I spent a few minutes checking his vehicle and documents and after giving him a warning about his speed, let him go on his way. He was so grateful not to have been booked due to him relying on being able to drive for his living. He was shaking my hand and thanking me profusely, saying that he would never forget my compassion. What he didn't know was that I wasn't able to report him for speeding anyway as my panda did not have a calibrated speedometer but he was so thankful that I thought it better not to divulge this bit of information in the interest of good police/public relations! A few weeks later I was at home with the kids, Kyri and Mark, when an ice cream van came into the street with a jingle playing to attract customers. I approached the window to purchase ice creams when who should appear from the inside of the van but, Joe, my speeding Italian man. He recognised me despite not being in uniform and grabbed my hand shaking it and thanking me again for letting him off. He refused to let me pay for the ice creams and each time Kyri or Mark and later on Stuart, went for an ice cream when I was at work, he wouldn't take their money. This would have gone on right up until we moved away from the area some forty-three years later if I hadn't put a stop to it. Every time I saw him to get ice creams he would say, "Hello my friend, I never forget you and what you did for me." I would reply, "Hello Joe, how are you and the family?" I would chat with him but made it clear that I would only get ice creams from him if I paid for them. If the kids were on their own, he would always ask, "How's your Dad?". A very nice man who I kept friendly with through the years.

Rye house had the go-cart track and also a speedway doubling as a greyhound racing track at this time and the place would be buzzing on a race day. On Sunday 8th September 1974 at 5.50 in the afternoon we were called to the speedway track as a young 9-year-old boy had gone missing. We got a description and began a search also making announcements over the public address system. After what seemed like a long time there was no sign, so we asked a couple of his friends with whom he had been playing to show us where they had been playing. They took us to the nearby river where there were two floating pontoons. The boys said they had been jumping from the bank onto the pontoon and then from one to the other. Although I still hoped that we would find the missing boy wandering about lost amongst the crowds a certain doubt crept in. Eventually, the underwater search team was summoned to search the river in the area of the pontoons. The boy was subsequently found at 2.30 a.m. wedged between the pontoons sadly drowned. I vividly remember the sadness of this tragic incident and how upset all of us involved in the search were.

There was a part of the ground that could only be reached by crossing a railway. On the other side was Dobbs Weir, which had a pub and a number of factories. If the crossing gates were shut, you either had to wait for the trains to pass or if an emergency, drive under the cattle creep at the side. A car would pass under this without a problem unless a car came from the other direction in which case one had to back up. Our panda cars at that time were Vauxhall Vivas' with a blue light on the top. This would just fit under the creep; however, a modification had been made to the panda one day that had a smart POLICE illuminated box under the blue light. Unfortunately, this was now too high to get under the cattle creep. A young constable, who shall remain nameless, was not aware of this however and whilst rushing to answer an alarm call in Dobbs Weir entered the cattle creep with the blue light flashing but came out the other end with no roof adornments. This incident caused much amusement amongst everyone at the station and the individual never lived it down.

Alarm calls were a regular happening and although I always made an effort to answer a central station alarm or if a member of the public informed us. There was rarely anything in it with most of these being due to technical problems with the systems or a gust of wind. However, at 10 p.m. on Monday 30th October 1972 the alarm went off at Woolworths store in the Tower Centre and when I got there, I found that the front door glass had been smashed. There was a hole big enough to climb through so I went inside to investigate. As I walked down the aisle towards the back of the store, I saw a figure creeping up the adjacent aisle. I waited until the figure got a bit closer and then leapt out shining my torch directly at the figure. The male, who was dressed in dark clothing and was holding something in his hands was so shocked to see me that he raised his hands in the air and said, "Ok it's a fair cop." It was the first and last time anyone was to say that to me. He was holding an alarm clock and it turned out that he was one cuckoo short of a clock himself. He ended up doing time – in a mental hospital!

People with mental health issues were not unusual to come across, especially since institutions had mostly been shut down in favour of 'care in the community'. One such person who came to notice on more than one occasion was, Steve, a local window cleaner, who, if he had forgotten to take his medication would run riot. It would take a few of us to subdue him on such occasions and struggle to get him back to the station. The next week you would see him in the town cleaning shop windows and he would wave and apologise for causing any trouble.

I remember that Fred and I had attended an alarm call at a factory premises about a mile from the station. There was nobody on the premises and once the keyholder had attended we decided to go back to the station for our break. As we were in separate pandas, I suggested that we should make the journey in reverse gear, which we did. There were many mad cap things that we did then most of which I couldn't possibly mention here.

I applied to join the Force's Tactical Patrol Group (TPG), which consisted of two personnel carriers each containing twelve officers, including a Sergeant. There was one for the Western side of the county and one for the East. The idea was that there was a dedicated group of officers that could be deployed or utilised at a moment's notice to any trouble spots in the county. There was always something going on somewhere and we were used for all manner of policing duties. Sometimes we would split up going out in pairs on foot or utilise any spare cars at the station we were visiting to patrol the area. We quelled many rowdy crowds, arrested numerous people for drugs and drink related offences, kept observations on buildings that were being targeted for criminal damage and attended Watford football ground on match days, amongst other things. On one occasion a couple of us were designated to keep observations on a school that was regularly being targeted by vandals. We were situated at the rear of the school in a field with little shelter on a freezing cold night. We were keeping as warm as we could under our capes, with a flask of soup to keep us going through the night. This was one assignment where we were unsuccessful in securing any arrests. A prime example of the fact that police work can sometimes be tiring, tedious, frustrating and not always exciting or successful.

On another occasion we were asked to give assistance with a problem that youths were causing in Hitchin. This was on Saturday 16th June 1973 at 10.30 in the evening. We split up and had officers patrolling the High Street in pairs. I was the designated driver of the carrier that night and my colleague and myself got some fish and chips and parked up quietly out of sight to enjoy them. Suddenly there was a call for urgent assistance from one of our group who had arrested someone for possession of drugs outside a pub in the Town Centre. The chips went flying and we sped into the High Street to be met by a crowd of dozens of people standing around outside a pub and right across the road. I managed to reach the spot where the officers were struggling with two prisoners and rushed to open the rear doors so we could get them in. The mob had other ideas and turned really nasty. We bundled the prisoners in the back after a struggle and I ran round to the driver's door to make a quick getaway. I was having to fight people off but I managed to get in and drive off. As I did so there was a rainstorm of beer glasses smashing on the carrier and all over the road around us. We made it away and back to the local police station, which at that time was a small building further down the High Street. The prisoners were taken into the station to be dealt with and shortly afterwards the mob that was at the pub had followed us to the station and we ended up under siege. Looking out of the window we could see that someone had cut the rope holding the flag that was flying outside. A couple of us would pop out and drag a couple of the mob in under suspicion of Criminal Damage and a few minutes later go and arrest a couple more. We ended up filing the cells before the crowd dispersed.

On another assignment to assist with rowdy gangs, on Friday night 13th July 1973, we went to my home station's ground in Hoddesdon. In the early hours of Saturday, a local dance turned out and youths were causing trouble with local residents. We were seriously outnumbered to start with and had to be satisfied with trying to keep order and usher the youths away from the town centre. I saw one of my mates being followed down the side of some shops known as the high path. There were about a dozen of them and they were spitting at him and shouting, *"BASTARD COPPER."* and, *"YOU BASTARD."* They continued to follow him, pushing him, spitting at him and shouting, *"WE'RE GOING TO KILL YOU, YOU BASTARD"* and *"WE'RE GOING TO FUCKING KILL YOU."* One of the youths approached him from the rear, kicked him at the top of his left leg and struck him in the face with his fist. Another youth was about to strike him when I ran up and grabbed the youth telling him that he was nicked. He struggled violently and managed to strike out with his fist hitting me on my nose and causing it to gush with blood. I managed to get him in a head lock and stop him from hitting me again. The group that were with this youth turned their attention to me and there was a lot of pushing, punching and shouting to try and free their mate. One was shouting, *"LET'S DO THE BASTARDS NOW, COME ON LET'S GET THEM."* Another said, *"LET GO OF HIM YOU FUCKING BASTARD OR I'LL KILL YOU."* This youth then struck me four times with his fists. I was not letting go however and still had a good hold of my prisoner around the neck. More pushing and fighting thrust us towards the shops and we ended up going through Dorothy Perkins plate glass shop window with me still having my prisoner in a headlock. We ended up rolling around amongst the display manikins and broken glass. Thankfully neither myself or my prisoner suffered from any cuts from the shards of glass all around us. Most youths ran off at this point as more troops started to arrive. My prisoner was conveyed back to the station as well as others that were gathered up nearby. I noticed that the youth who had struck me in the face was amongst these so he was charged with assaulting me occasioning actual bodily harm as well as affray. He had the nerve to accuse me of beating him up in the cells, which I hasten to add was not true. There was a full investigation and after a forensic examination of the cell where he had been kept, it was found that he had split open his own lip and smeared blood on the walls himself. He and his mates ended up with sentences up to 3 months at a borstal and I got a Chief Constable's commendation.

Not all situations or duties were as manic as this however and a lot of the time we were engaged in drug related searches. There was a growing drug problem within Hertfordshire at the time and we were raiding premises with warrants plus stopping and searching individuals in the street. A colleague and myself stopped a male in the street one day (I can't recall where exactly) to check him out. Something about him was not right and my colleague decided to search him. Nothing was found in his outer clothing but not being entirely satisfied we decided to detain him for a more thorough search at the station. He was conveyed to the station and the Sergeant in the charge room gave consent for a strip search. He was taken to a cell where he removed his clothes until he was down to his underpants. Nothing was found in his clothes and he was told to remove his underpants, nothing apparent there either. I have to say that at this stage I thought that we had got it wrong about this individual. However, he was told to squat and as he did so a piece of silver foil fell to the floor from his parted bum cheeks. There was a substantial amount of white powder inside the foil wrap which was subsequently found to be cocaine. A great find for us, a bit of a bummer for him!

I was attached to the TPG for 12 months and would have applied for an extension but for the fact that they had decided that we should receive firearms training and subsequently carry weapons. I did not find this prospect appealing so left the group and went back to Hoddesdon to resume normal duties.

At the start of each early turn or late turn day shifts the Sergeant would assign you with a handful of enquiries to complete. These would range from central ticket office enquiries, requests from other forces to obtaining witness statements, warrants of arrest to execute and warrants to collect money, to name but a few. You never knew what you would get and were expected to deal with all enquiries either that day or within a week. I always carried a clipboard in the panda with statement forms, accident report books and receipt books for collecting unpaid fines. I would knock on the door of a person who owed money to the court and as they hadn't paid a warrant was issued requiring the person named to pay up or be arrested. Once identified as the person named on the warrant, I could say those classic words, "It's the money or you." It was usually the money but sometimes them.

The central ticket office was in London and they would send out enquiries requesting a visit to a registered owner to establish who was the driver at the time a vehicle had been given a parking ticket. If established that the person spoken to was the offender they would be reported and the paperwork sent back to the central ticket office. I called at one house to speak to a suspected offender and saw that there was a long skewer with chunks of lamb cooking over a home-made bar-B-Q in the garage at the side of the house. I spoke to the man doing the cooking and introduced myself. He was very friendly and immediately welcomed me to his house and offered me a drink. I told him why I was at his door and that it would not be appropriate for me to accept a drink. He asked me what it was all about and I established that he was the person I had to report. He admitted that he was and said that now that had been dealt with, I must have a drink. I was ushered into his house, introduced to his wife and treated like a VIP guest. Out came a glass of beer and a bowl of nuts and cherries placed on the table in front of me. The family were Greek Cypriots and as with most Greek Cypriots, very pro-police. We had a great chat and I was told that I must try a glass of their special Greek Brandy. In the interest of good Police/public relations, how could I refuse!

A short time later there was a knock at the door and their expected guests had arrived. I thanked them for their hospitality and said that I would leave them to enjoy their family Bar-B-Q. "Where do you think you're going, you're staying to have some food with us." The next thing I knew I was seated at the head of their dining table with all the family gathered round, chatting with me and plying me with more drink. That was an enquiry I had no trouble dealing with! When I got back to the station the Sergeant said, "Where the hell have you been?" "Just dealing with my enquiries Sarge."

The Chief Inspector in charge at Hoddesdon was a strict, but fair, Scotsman who stood no nonsense but could be seen as being a bit eccentric on occasions. You were only allowed back to the station once during your tour of duty and that was for your 45-minute refreshment period. One day I had dealt with an accident in the pouring rain and had popped back to the station to write up my accident report book in the dry. The Chief Inspector came into the office and said, "What are you doing in here?" I said, "Writing up an accident report book sir." He replied, "Out on the street is the place to do that, out!" On another occasion I was relieving the station duty officer covering the phones and front counter. I had left the lost property cupboard door open whilst answering the phone and I suddenly heard a barking sound coming from the direction of the front office and lost property cupboard. The Chief Inspector walked in to where I was and said, "What's that damned dog doing in here?" I said, "What dog sir?" "The one in the lost property cupboard, you'd better go and get it out." I went to the cupboard and looking in could see no dog in sight. The next thing I knew I was shoved into the cupboard and the door was shut and locked behind me. All I could hear then was hoots of laughter from the Chief Inspector as he walked away. I was let out a short time later by the SDO returning from his refreshments.

A gentleman called the station one day to say that he was in France on a wine buying trip and had, before leaving home turned off his electric and gas supplies at his flat. He then realised that he needed to leave his gas fridge switched on to protect some wine and so turned his supplies back on. His fear was that he had not then re-lit the pilot light in the fridge, thereby allowing gas to build up in the flat and a danger of explosion. I was designated to attend the flat and assess the situation. I attended with a colleague, established that the flat was on the first floor and also that the door was securely locked with no window by the side of it. We looked round the back of the premises and could see no easy access there either, so I decided that we would have to break down the door. This we did, leaving the splintered door and frame severely damaged but did get inside, opened the windows and switched off the gas. We then got a boarding up service to come along and secure the premises after we had turned the gas back on and lit the pilot light once again.

A week later I was on front desk duty when the owner of the flat came in to pay the bill of the boarding up service. I thought that he might make a complaint about the officer who had smashed down his door so I kept quiet that it was me. However, he produced a bottle of wine and said he wanted to thank the officer very much and that his expensive wine in his fridge had been saved as a result. I, of course, admitted that it was me, accepted his gratitude and the bottle of wine! Another exercise in police/public relations!

Another case of a reported missing person came late one summers evening from a lock house on the River Lea. I attended the scene with a Sergeant to establish the facts and get a description. There had been a party at the lock house with the people at the party quite obviously having consumed vast quantities of alcohol. A few of the party goers had decided that it would be a good idea to cool off by having a dip in the water between the lock gates so had stripped off and dived in. It was shortly after this that one of the party had gone missing and nobody could say where he was, but he had been one of the bathers. The Sergeant and I looked at each other and came to the obvious conclusion that he must still be in the lock. We got some rope and tied an old starting handle in the middle to act as a weight. The Sergeant was one side of the river and I was on the other bank. Between us we sunk the rope to the bottom of the lock and dragged it along to see if we could feel any obstructions. On one haul, when we lifted the rope, an arm appeared hanging over the rope. Unfortunately, it was not there for very long and slipped back under the water. Out came the underwater search team and recovered the body.

Whilst on desk duty one day an elderly gentleman came in with a Home Office Road Traffic form 1 (HORT1 'Producer') together with his driving documents. A **producer** is issued when you are unable to produce driving documents to a police officer immediately. You are then required to nominate a police station at which to produce your documents within 7 days. The documents were in order but also very unusually it also had on the form a handwritten extra asking for the person producing the documents to be given an eyesight test. I duly took the gentleman outside having to assist him as he was having difficulty walking and very frail. I pointed him towards a car that was approximately 25 yards away and asked him to read me the registration number. "What car?" was the reply. It would appear that he had been involved in an accident where it was alleged that he had driven straight through a red traffic light at a junction and collided with another car. I told him that the result of the test would be reported back to the officer concerned and he then said that he would no longer be driving and I could have the contents of his post office savings account if I didn't report him for failing the eye test. I declined his offer but did give him a lift to the Town as his taxi had left and that's where he wanted to go. I never did find out how much I had turned down but did find out that he was summoned to appear at court for dangerous driving amongst other offences. He never made it to court, however and died a short time later.

My first appearance at Cheshunt Magistrates is something I will never forget and was deeply embarrassing. I have no idea why I am revealing it now? At training school in mock-up court room exercises we were taught to finish off by saying, "And that your worships is my evidence." On this occasion, although nervous, I gave my evidence clearly and was pleased to have given it without a hitch. At the end I said, "And that your evidence is my worships". All the other officers at the back of the court together with the others present and the Magistrates burst into laughter and I turned bright red! I never gave the suggested phrase at the end of giving evidence again.

I was aware that there was a tendency for officers to embellish their evidence at times and maybe even bend the truth. I couldn't possibly say whether I ever resorted to such methods. However, I can say that I never stitched anyone up and always played the game fairly. Yes, sometimes it was a game between the regular villains and the local cops. I never really got upset if the bad guys won on occasions as I knew that their time would eventually come. I do recall one time when I did get annoyed though. On Monday 22nd April 1974 at 6.10p.m. I was driving my panda along Station Road, Broxbourne approaching the junction with the High Road. I saw a single decker bus coming from my left along the High Road heading towards Hoddesdon. It was going quite slowly as it approached the lights, they turned to red against it. Although the driver had plenty of time to stop, he continued straight through the red signal and stopped at the bus stop just a short distance from the junction. The bus then proceeded towards Hoddesdon. I followed at a speed of 40m.p.h. and eventually caught him as he stopped at a bus stop in the High Street. I pointed out the offence to him and he said that he thought it was dangerous to stop at the lights. I told him what speed he was doing and said, "I suppose you are behind schedule?" He said, "Yes as a matter of fact I am." As far as I was concerned it was a blatant disregard for the traffic law and I had no hesitation in reporting him for the offence. He pleaded not guilty and off we went to the Magistrates Court. As far as I was concerned the evidence was clear cut and it was his word against mine. I gave my evidence clearly and concisely, without embellishing the facts. He was represented by a solicitor from the bus company and in the witness box said that he thought the lights had changed to amber and that it was too dangerous to stop. The next thing I knew he was calling a witness who was apparently a passenger in the bus at the time. The passenger said that he observed the lights at amber as the bus approached the junction, backing up the driver's account. I can tell you that it was the most blatant case of failing to stop at a red light I have ever seen. Even though it was established under cross examination that the passenger also worked as a driver for the bus company, the magistrates decided to give the defendant the benefit of the doubt. There, now it's off my chest reader and I can get on with the rest of my story.

I think now is the time to add a tale involving nudity. It was on Saturday 6th July 1974 at 3.15 in the morning when I was patrolling the town centre in company with a Sergeant. I suddenly saw a moped and a motor scooter pass along the road with riders who were naked apart from crash helmets. I followed them and eventually caught up with them in a lane just off the end of the High Street. When I pulled up and got out of the car, I found two youths behind a fence, both naked apart from crash helmets. There were two bundles of clothes on the ground next to where they were standing. I immediately identified them as male. I'd like to say that it stuck out a mile but actually it didn't. We told them to put their clothes on and separated them to question them. After a couple of minutes, the Sergeant came over to consult with me and the other youth ran off. The youth who I was talking to also tried to run off but I got hold of him and whilst talking to him several other youths appeared on the scene. I placed the youth into the panda and he turned stroppy, trying to get out of the car on the other side and struggling with us. He was taken back to the station completely denying that it was him riding naked through the streets of Hoddesdon. He was charged with conduct likely to cause a Breach of the Peace as there wasn't an offence on the statute books to cover bare back riding on a motor scooter.

I did learn during the first few years in the force that there were some really unsavoury characters, some ignorant and thoroughly nasty people and some that defy description. We had arrested a man one day on suspicion of burglary and went to his house to search it for the proceeds of the burglary. Present at the property were his wife and a young 18-month-old baby. The house was extremely dirty and untidy, although untidy did not really describe the poor state it was in. In the kitchen all the sides were covered in discarded food containers and dirty crockery and cutlery. The sink was overflowing with unclean pots and pans and heaven knows what. There were several part-used bottles of milk dotted around, which were in various states of decay, making the place stink of sour milk. When we went upstairs the stench was unbearable and searching through the rooms was quite traumatic. In the bathroom the toilet was obviously blocked with excreta filling the pan and because of that they had started using the bath. In what must have been the, "Nursery", there was just a cot on one side, on bare floorboards, which had a urine sodden mattress and no bed clothes. In the corner of the room was a pile of dirty and sodden terry towelling nappies which had been used and then left in the room and added to. The smell was off the scale and steam was rising from them. We found the stolen property in the attic (probably the cleanest spot in the whole house) so the man was further arrested. In addition, we decided to take the baby into care and got the social services involved because it was clear to see that there was a need to remove it to a place of safety. I found out later that after the social services got the mother to clean the place up, they handed the child back. I often wondered what happened to that baby? Probably went to University and ended up as a Chief Constable somewhere!?

There were a lot of raids on banks around this time, which is why it was decided to put an increased uniform patrol in town centres. On one occasion I was designated to perform foot patrol in Hertford Town Centre. The main street where the banks were situated was not very long so it could get a bit boring just walking up and down. It was therefore a welcome relief when a very attractive young lady came up to me and engaged in a conversation. She was very friendly and said that she liked talking to the police who were regularly patrolling the town. She said that she would like to meet up with me after duty one night and gave me her phone number. I couldn't believe my luck and told my mates back at the hostel later that day. "Oh her," was the response, "She chats up all the guys on bank patrol and is looking to get one into bed." I said, "Well she has given me her number so I might give her a call." "You do know that she is only 15, don't you?" Well you could have knocked me over with a feather because she definitely looked a lot older than that. Needless to say, I did not ring her, nor did I volunteer for bank patrol in Hertford again.

Police vehicles back in the 70's were pretty basic and none more so than the Divisional transport. This was a Bedford Dormobile with wooden slatted seats in the back, the same one that we used to transport prisoners to Brixton, Pentonville and Holloway prisons. It was also used to transport us to Stansted airport when there was a full emergency. This didn't happen often but Herts Police acted as support to Essex Police should there be a major incident at the airport. If a call came in that there was a full emergency, usually a plane with a fault in its landing gear, anyone who was on duty would be picked up by the divisional transport and we would set off hell for leather towards the Stansted major incident rendezvous point. The distance to cover was approximately 25 miles and would take about half an hour with a full load of 10 coppers in a Bedford Dormobile. The challenge was to reach the rendezvous point before we got the message, "Stand down." We never did make it to the designated point and thankfully there was never a crash.

Up until 1972, the most serious crimes were tried at the Assizes, after being committed there by the Quarter Sessions, so called because they were held four times a year. These were held in Hertford and because security was of high importance I, together with others, would be designated to be present in the building during trials. I witnessed some interesting cases during my postings there and picked up some very useful tips about giving evidence. I recall my Chief Inspector being required to give evidence in a shooting case and was being challenged in the witness box by a defence barrister. He was accusing him of lying on oath after it was established that a fact that had been related contradicted his evidence. "Are you calling my client a liar officer?". "No, sir I am saying he is mistaken." A classic response in my books and one I never forgot. This style of courts was abolished by the Courts Act 1971 and replaced by a single permanent Crown Court.

I never kept a count of my arrests or persons reported during my time as a PC in Hertfordshire Constabulary but there was a fair few. I made arrests for Burglary, Theft, Criminal Damage, Affray, Assault, Disqualified Driving and Drunk & Disorderly to name a few. I reported people for a variety of traffic offences and also such heinous offences as: – No lights on a bike, No dog licence and no pedlar's certificate.

Chapter 8 – Girls and Marriage

As well as many difficult and testing times between 1970 and 1974 there were also a lot of fun times shared with friends and colleagues. I remained close friends with Colin and Fred and I was with them when they met their respective girlfriends, later to become their wives. Colin's girlfriend, Janice, worked in a shop in the centre of Hertford and we would quite often go in there on the pretence of looking at the merchandise, so Colin could chat with her. Fred's girlfriend was Gill although I called her Gillikins and I played gooseberry many times during their courtship. Fred and I decided that we would drive up to Scotland for a holiday and to visit his parents.

As we were on a tight budget, we borrowed a large metal framed tent from one of our tea stops. In fact, this was from the lady at the dry cleaners in Hoddesdon. Off we went shoving everything into my bright red Austin 1100 car that I had at that time (MUR 799D). Fred had originated from Paisley so we headed there first and arrived early one morning calling at one of his old mates. The first thing we did was to have a beer from his fridge. After visiting friends and later his parents, we went to his old cricket club where it was decided that we would pitch our tent later that night. After a few beers we went to a party round someone's house where more beer was consumed. I had a few too many to drive back to the cricket ground, so Fred took on the task and drove us. I had to tell him to stop on the way as I was feeling decidedly ill and just made it from the car to a shop front before I was decidedly sick. Fred shouted at me to get back in the car quickly as he had espied a copper walking along the main road towards us. I got back in the car and as Fred pulled away the officer stopped us. He asked if we had been drinking and Fred said, "He has but I have nay." "There are public conveniences for being sick in." "Sorry officer, I got taken short, it won't happen again." "Make sure it doesn't, on your way." We went quickly before he changed his mind and smelt Fred's breath, which must have reeked as much as mine, having consumed as much beer as I had during the day.

I think we both breathed a very big sigh of relief and we quickly made our way to the cricket field. I've no recollection of how and all I remember was being woken later that day by some of Fred's mates who were laughing at the partly and wrongly constructed tent that was just covering us. It taught me a valuable lesson that when staying in a tent that requires a technical degree to construct the many metal poles and huge canvas covering, then you should do so before you go out and consume vast quantities of beer. We packed up all our stuff and proceeded to drive out of the field but with difficulty as there were huge ruts to negotiate. I said, "We are never going to be able to drive this car out of here." Fred said, "Well we drove it in here last night." The rest of that week was spent driving around some lovely countryside including, Loch Lomond, Fort William, Applecross and Ayr. When we reached Ayr, we parked on a beach and had to dig a pit under the car in order to do a running repair to the exhaust, which had developed a rattle. It was a great week and after we had toured along the West coast of Scotland, we headed to North Wales to meet up with Gillikins and her family who were holidaying there. It was a good holiday, with me playing gooseberry again but also keeping out the way when Fred and Gill wanted time on their own.

Dave, who was on the same shift as me and also lived in the hostel had a girlfriend, Denise, who I got to know but not as closely as the others. I was somewhat surprised when Dave asked me to be best man at his wedding, but accepted gladly. I recall that just a few days before the wedding, Dave and I went to a pitch and putt ground in Hertford. Dave struck his ball at the first tee and I said, "Stand back, I'll show you how it's done." I took an almighty swing, missed the ball and as the club went full circle over my shoulder, I struck Dave splitting open the skin above his eye. He had to have stitches and Denise was not best pleased with me to say the least, especially as I was supposed to be looking after him leading up to the wedding. They got married on 9th September 1972 in Hertford.

Colin and Jan got married in September 1973 and Fred was his best man. Fred and Gill got married in July 1974, with Colin being his best man. I had dated a girl called Katherine, who lived in Welwyn Garden City, I can't remember what she did but I spent a fair bit of time with her and she was really nice. I'm not sure why and when we parted but I then met Christine, who was a radio dispatcher in the control room at Police Headquarters. We weren't particularly well suited but had lots of fun and when she moved to Fulham, I used to drive all the way to London to see her. That didn't last for long, although there were benefits in making the journey the disadvantages outweighed these and we split up.

One of the guys in the Hostel, Steve, and I got a contact in an electrical shop in Hoddesdon to make us a twin deck disco machine with two huge speakers. After spending some money on the latest records, we offered our services in running a disco at private functions. I could get the twin deck and one speaker on the back seat and one speaker in the boot of my latest car, a Vauxhall Victor Mk II which I purchased from a Sergeant at the station for £300 (GEV 300B). One booking we had was at a caravan site next to the new A10 dual carriageway by-pass that was under development. The caravans were for the workers building the roadway and they had a large communal hall on the site for us to run our disco. I had found out about this opportunity through one of the workers daughters, June, who I had gone out with for a short period. On Tuesday 15th May 1973, the night of the disco, a girl I knew who worked in a shop in Hoddesdon High Street, Jane, came up to me and asked if I would dance with her sister. I actually knew her sister by sight and to wave to if I saw her out pushing a pram with her two children. She was married but separated from her husband who had been a Police Constable at the station, albeit on a different shift. He had controversially left her some 7 months previously for another woman and at the same time resigned from the police.

Anyway, Jane said that her sister, Barbara was feeling a bit low and it was her first outing since her husband had left her, so would I try and cheer her up by asking her to dance. I was happy to oblige and very much enjoyed her company. At the end of the night I gave Jane and Barbara a lift home and said that I was going to a party the night after next that usually lasted all night and would they like to come with me. Jane persuaded Barbara to go with me saying that she would baby-sit for her. So it was that on the night of Thursday 17th May 1973 I picked up Barbara and off we went to Eve's celebrated all night party. It was a short time into the evening that Barbara had consumed a fair amount of alcohol in a rapid amount of time. She was taken to an upstairs bedroom to sleep it off, leaving me to carry on as normal socialising and drinking with my mates. Two or three hours later Barbara came back downstairs feeling better and we got to dancing and then talking. Whilst we were dancing to a slower record something strange happened and all of a sudden, we were locked in a passionate embrace and began kissing. I think it was from that moment that I knew Barbara was the girl for me and we spent ages walking round Eve's garden just talking. I saw and spoke to Barbara on a daily basis from that day also getting to know her lovely children.

Kyri was the eldest at 4 and Mark was the youngest at 17 months. Did I think that I was going to be the one bringing them up? Probably not, all I knew was that I wanted to be with Barbara, everything else was initially superfluous. On 24th March 1974 I proposed to Barbara whilst we were at her school friend's wedding reception and on 26th April 1974 Barbara was legally divorced. Two weeks later, we went to Hatton Garden to get an engagement ring and a week after that we had an engagement party at my parent's house. Originally when I told them about Barbara, the fact that she was still married to someone else and had two children, I can only say that they were not best pleased. "I never thought you would bring trouble home to this house." And "Don't bring that woman round here." Were two responses from my Mum. However once that they saw I was serious they finally came round and were fine from that day onwards.

We decided to get married sooner rather than later so set a date of 26th October 1974. As Barbara was a divorcee, we could not get married in a Church of England premises. This was something that really rankled with me for two reasons. Firstly, I had not been married before and secondly, Barbara was an innocent party in the break-up of her marriage. Since then I have had no time for C of E and their outdated and stuffy attitude. However, my Sister, Moira, was a Methodist and through her I knew a vicar at the church in Ordnance Road, Enfield. He agreed that we could marry at his church and so it was on 26th October

1974 that we got married. Fred was our best man and Barbara's brother Richard gave her away. Her Dad, Jack, was unfortunately at that time in hospital with Tuberculosis (TB) and not allowed to attend the wedding. Barbara and I made all the arrangements and paid for most of it on a tight budget. Our wedding car was a Rover owned and driven by Cyril (he of the hole in the wall club), who took us to the hospital to see Barbara's Dad on the way to the reception. Apart from our families I think that the majority of Hoddesdon Police station attended. I still have receipts for the following:-

For all the flowers - £7.50
Catering for wedding reception for 70 people - £137.12 (paid for by Barbara's Dad, Jack)
My wedding ring - £14
My Suit - £29.25
Hire of Hall for reception - £15.50
Barbara's Dress - £19.95

We blew all the other money I had saved up, on a week's honeymoon to Majorca. Barbara's Dad and sister looked after the children whilst we flew off from Stansted airport, then just a small affair. It was the first time I had flown and the first time going abroad. I was absolutely petrified on the flight out, especially every time there was a sudden drop or shuddering due to headwind or air pockets. I was never so happy to set foot on terra firma when we reached Majorca. I had to have a few glasses of brandy to calm my nerves for the flight back. When we got back Kyri and Mark started calling me Dad after Jane had told them that I was now their Dad. Although I was strict with them and stood no nonsense, I like to think that I was a good Dad and certainly loved them very much.

It was as a result of my marriage to Barbara that I was to part company with Hertfordshire Constabulary. In the early 1970's the Chief Constable had to be informed of changes of circumstances and approve the address where a Constable would be living. It was therefore on 30th July 1974 that I submitted a report to the Chief Superintendent informing him of my intention to marry and move into the council house where Barbara and the children were now living. Barbara had been living in a police house with her first husband when he left her and so she was now subject to being evicted to allow a serving officer to occupy the property. In October 1973 Barbara was evicted and placed by the council in a house in Broxbourne. The reply came back from above that I would not be allowed to move into this address as it was not police policy to allow a serving officer to live in a council house and that I should apply for a police house. Being unaware of the politics going on in the background, I did apply for a police house and requested one in Hoddesdon. I was told that I would be allocated a house in Hertford, to where I would be transferred on the date of my marriage.

We were not happy with this but did go and look at the house. It had obviously been vacant for months and apart from the smell of damp and mildew it was in dire need of complete decoration. It was after this visit that I decided enough was enough and put in an application to transfer to the Metropolitan Police. The Chief Inspector called me into his office and tried to talk me out of this move saying that I could not hold the Assistant Chief Constable to ransom. I said that I wasn't really expecting to get accepted as I expected that somebody from Herts would inform the Met and put a block on my application. He said that they wouldn't do such a thing but I said, "Oh yes they would." I was resigned to having to look for another job.

It was not an easy decision to make and I certainly did not want to leave Hertfordshire Constabulary and all my mates. I found out subsequently that there were several empty Police houses in Herts and that the Chief Constable was under pressure to fill. My timing was poor and I was being taken for a mug.

Chapter 9 - Transferring to the MET

It was in September that I received a letter asking me to attend the Metropolitan Police careers information and selection centre in Harrow Road, London right next to Paddington Green police station, on 3rd October 1974. There were three high ranking officers on the panel and they asked lots of questions about Barbara, her former husband, the children and the property in which she was living. They stated that I would be expected to work at a busy London police station and not expect to be able to be posted at an outlying division. I told them that I had always intended to transfer to the Metropolitan Police, I wanted the experience of working at a busy London police station and was prepared to move to wherever they deemed to post me.

None of this was true but my past experiences had taught me that when dealing with senior officers you always told them what they wanted to hear. After a real grilling I was not very optimistic in my application, they certainly didn't appear very encouraging towards me and told me to go and wait in the canteen. A short time later a young lady came and requested that I follow her to another office. There she told me that I had been successful in my application and would make the necessary arrangements with Hertfordshire Constabulary for my transfer. When I asked about where I would be living, she asked me what arrangements I had at that time. I told her that I was getting married later that month and had intended moving into a council house where my future wife was already living. She asked me the address, checked that it was within the permitted radius of 25 miles from Charring Cross (the boundary at that time) and said, "That's no problem we will pay the rent on that."

I was flabbergasted and further stunned when I later found out where I was to be posted. I reported to New Scotland Yard on 9th December 1974 to be attested into the Metropolitan Police together with a bunch of new recruits and several other transferees. The recruits then got on a coach to travel to Hendon training school and the rest of us had to wait in reception for our divisional transport to pick us up. A short time later a car and driver turned up and we were off to my new posting. I asked the driver, "Where are we going?" He said, "Wood Green." Oh, dear was my thought, I know it was probably the nearest busy station but some distance from home. "No, you're not being stationed there we are just going to see the Commander so that he can welcome you to the area. After that we are off to Enfield." That was a much better station for me and nearer to home. "No, you're not being stationed there either we are just going to see the Divisional Chief Superintendent so that he can welcome you to the Division." "Oh, so where am I actually going to be stationed then?" I asked. "Cheshunt!" He said. Well I was lost for words and couldn't believe my luck. I knew the area well and it was on the border between my old station, Hoddesdon and was the first station in the Met area. All my old colleagues at Hoddesdon couldn't help calling me a jammy person, or words to that effect. I was living in the house where the Assistant Chief Constable of Herts. had said I could not live, getting paid more money plus a London allowance and right on my doorstep. "The Assistant Chief Constable has really screwed you hasn't he!" Was one comment.

I settled in to life at Cheshunt very quickly and found that a lot of the procedures and attitudes were easier and more relaxed than I was used to. On my first trip out with one of the Constables on my shift, all of whom were a lot older than I, said, "How come someone as young as you has managed to get posted to Cheshunt, most of us are here to see out the last years of our service after working in central London, are you sick, lame or lazy?"

Chapter 10 – Ponders Plonk

However, after only four months at Cheshunt there was a requirement for two officers to transfer to Ponders End police station, the next station along, as they were short of Constables and it was a busier station. It was a question of last in, first out, so off I went to spend the next 9 years at Ponders End, or Ponders Plonk as it was endearingly referred to. Again, I knew the ground well as some of it was where I grew up and went to school. I was back to my roots! My parents still lived in Holmesdale and that was handy as I could drop in for a cuppa and a chat. Holmesdale was affectionately referred to at that time as 'Bread Pudding Lane,' as there was always a tray of bread pudding to offer me and anyone I had with me.

Here I joined a relief with two Sergeants and 8 Constables, on paper. Quite often we were reduced to one Sergeant and between 4 and 6 P.C.s. These years as a P.C. were always busy and the ground that we covered was varied between, medium to low value housing, high rise blocks, commercial factories and shops. I will relate some remembered incidents from those years here although I can't guarantee the correct order of when they happened.

Drugs didn't appear to be such a problem in the mid-seventies and most incidents were petty theft, shoplifting, taking a vehicle without consent (TWOC), burglary, criminal damage, domestic disputes, sudden deaths and drink driving amongst others.

I attended many premises, both residential and commercial that had been burgled. Some were ransacked and some just turned over sufficiently to find the stuff worth stealing. Burglars most certainly had no regard for other people's property and often caused more damage to the property than the worth of the goods that were stolen. On more than one occasion I found human excreta in the corner of a room, where the burglar felt a need to relieve himself. I recall attending one house where the owner had returned home to find their house had been burgled. I established the point of entry and went through each room taking a note of things disturbed or items missing. I went into an upstairs bedroom and came across complete devastation. There were clothes strewn all over the room and drawers were left open with proceeds scattered over the bed. I said to the owner that it was sad that the burglar would make such a mess. He said, "Actually this is our teenage daughter's room and they haven't been in here. This is what it normally looks like."

I was called to a chemist's shop one day where a male in his twenties was trying to obtain prescription drugs on a forged prescription. I attended and challenged the man outside the shop where he immediately stuffed a piece of paper in his mouth and tried to swallow it. I instantly and foolishly thrust my fingers in his mouth to prevent him swallowing and to retrieve what I presumed to be the evidence. After rolling about on the pavement for a short time with a small crowd of onlookers gathered round, I managed to retrieve a soggy mass of paper and after managing to open it out, found it to be a portion of a charge sheet from a previous time he had been arrested. That was the last time I went anywhere near an open mouth and was thankful I didn't lose any fingers. I also learned that if you are expecting any members of the public to assist you, it is highly unlikely to happen. Needless to say, he was arrested and charged with attempting to obtain property by deception.

Domestic disputes were common place and I learnt that once you attended the scene to try and sort out a problem that has probably been building up over a number of months, or in some cases years, there is no way you are going to solve it in a few minutes. Quite often both parties would turn their vitriol and hate towards you, so that when you left, they would be talking to each other but hating the police for interfering. These were always a no-win situation, although in some more extreme cases you would have to arrest someone. I attended a house one day with another older, more experienced and old-style P.C. We knocked on the door and a woman answered it displaying a nasty black eye. Her husband had come home from the pub and when she remonstrated with him for being out too long and his dinner being ruined, he hit her. As she was telling us this a voice from inside said, *"And you can fuck off it's got fuck all to do with you."* The P.C. with me pushed past the woman went into the lounge and dragged the husband out of the house shoving him into the back of the police car. "Next time don't tell me it's got fuck all to do with me." The man apologised profusely, we took him to stay at his parents for the night and I never got called to that address again.

On another occasion I was on my own and knocking at the door of a house I heard a woman shouting and screaming. I knocked louder and announced who I was whereupon the woman shouted, "Don't come in he's got a knife and he's going to stab the first copper who comes through the door." I took out my truncheon, my only means of defence, and held it behind my back in readiness. The door was opened and sure enough a man was just inside waving a large kitchen knife about and shouting threats. I kept talking to him for what seemed like ages and eventually managed to persuade him to hand over the knife. I took him back to the station under arrest and after he calmed down, he was released without charge as his wife refused to press or substantiate any charges.

Ponders End Police Station was on the High Street and the ground floor window where we met up for tea and briefings overlooked the road. On a bright sunny summer evening we were having said tea break and admiring the young ladies passing by in their skimpy summer outfits. There was one walking along that had an extremely skimpy outfit with a very short skirt and a comment from one of the lads was, "Will you look at the way she's dressed, it's no wonder that these women get raped." The next minute she was entering the front counter at the station and alleging that she had just been raped.

I took a description of the alleged attacker and we began an immediate search of the area, C.I.D. were informed and all the forensic procedures took place. Some weeks later the person responsible was identified, arrested and charged with rape. I gave evidence at the Old Bailey in relation to this case, the only time I appeared there, although I spent a lot of time at other courts. I will relate some more court stories a bit later.

One of the rooms on the ground floor at the station was the collator's office. He was the person to go to for information on local villains and generally unsociable law-breaking types. Pictures of wanted people were displayed on the wall plus the more prolific local offenders and those suspected of committing crimes. Whilst looking through the pictures one day I spied a face that I recognised from the past. There was Micky Draper staring out at me, that awful school bully from years before and the information was that he was a disqualified driver suspected of still using his van. So, I did a 'recce' early one morning to see if I could see his vehicle and lo and behold, I found it just round the corner from his address. I settled back out of sight in my panda and waited.

After a long wait, the van came round the corner and continued towards the main road. I followed as I couldn't see who was driving at that stage. As I got to the junction, I saw Micky parking up and going into a newsagent's shop. As he came out, I approached him and put it to him that he was driving whilst disqualified. He emphatically denied driving saying that he was a passenger and his mate was driving. I invited him to join me in the back of the panda whilst I did a confirmatory check on his disqualification. The reply came back that he was indeed disqualified. On the way back to the police station he said, "I know you, don't I?" I replied, "Do you?" He said, "You used to go to Albany, didn't you?" I replied, "As a matter of fact I did." He said, "I've changed a lot since those days." I replied, "Yes and so have I, you're nicked!" Probably one of the more satisfying arrests I have made and just goes to prove that it is true what they say, 'What goes round, comes round!'

An occupational hazard of being a police officer is having complaints made against you. I had very few during my career and none that were justified. The first one was made by the lad who accused me of beating him up in the cell, which was forensically proved to be malicious. My second was when I was posted as Station Officer in June of 1980 at Ponders End. Someone alleged that he had produced his documents at the front counter but that the officer who was there did not make an official record and just said, "That's OK". He was subsequently summoned to appear at court for no test certificate and failing to produce it. I was served with a notice of complaint (known as a 163) because I was the designated Station Officer that day. I have no idea if anyone had dealt with this chap on that day but it certainly wasn't me and I suspect that he had made it up in an attempt to get the summonses against him dropped. The best form of defence being to attack. I was subsequently absolved of any involvement after an investigation.

The panda car I drove for most of the time was an Austin Allegro or as we called it, 'the Austin All aggro'. It was not built for speed and not really suitable in a pursuit type situation. However, I can recall a couple of incidents when I had occasion to give chase. One was after an emergency call that there had been a serious domestic incident and the husband who had badly assaulted his wife had fled the scene in his car. I drove to the vicinity to keep an eye out for the vehicle described together with Julie, a Woman Police Constable. We spotted the car and got behind it with a view to stopping it. He had other ideas and led us on a chase around the surrounding streets.

After a few minutes of screeching tyres and hair raising near misses he abandoned his car in the middle of a side road and ran off. I stopped the panda and got out to chase him on foot, leaving my car door open and Julie following several feet behind me. He was quite a way ahead of me but I still had sight of him and kept going, throwing my cap into someone's front garden on the way. As I got to the High Road, I just saw him ducking behind a lorry parked up on the opposite side of the road. I pressed on and as I got to where I had last seen him, I found him doubled up behind the lorry gasping for breath. My running training had paid off and after arresting the suspect for assault I walked him back towards the panda. On the way we met the out-of-breath Julie, holding my discarded cap. She said, "I can't believe how quick you were out of the panda, you were like grease lightening."

Women police have not featured much in my story and perhaps I should give a brief account of my personal experience of them. When I first joined the police in Herts, there were very few female officers and those that there were looked after women prisoners and young children. They did not generally work nights and were not paid the same as their male counterparts. Things improved and, in the Met, we had women police on most reliefs. Attitudes were changing but there was still a large body of opinion that women were the fairer sex and should be nurtured and protected. However, there was still a culture that existed that women needed to be initiated as one of the 'gang'. This consisted of the station stamp being applied to bare buttocks. I have to say that

I was neither party to or witness to such an event but am sure from stories related to me that it happened quite a lot.

One WPC we had on our relief for a long time and before Julie, was Carolyn. She was so used to people mispronouncing her name as Caroline that she would say, "It's Carolyn actually." So, from that day we always referred to her as 'Carolyn actually'. She was from a very good family, was well educated and talked with a posh accent. She was lovely, very good at the job and I'm sure would never allow herself to suffer the indignity of the station stamp on her nether regions.

Another car chase was to happen at the end of a very uneventful night duty. I was driving the 'All aggro' sedately along the Hertford Road towards the nick for a last cup of tea before booking off duty at 6am. Sitting beside me was Brian, the Sergeant, who was nodding off. Suddenly a Mk II Rover came past me from behind at a bit more than the 30m.p.h. speed limit. Not being a stickler for people doing a bit more than they should on a quiet road in the early hours, I wasn't too bothered but thought that it was a bit cheeky to overtake a marked police vehicle and decided to follow him for a bit. As I got a bit closer, he seemed to speed up and we got faster and faster. It was obvious that he had no desire to be stopped and Brian was now wide awake and shouting on the radio for a fast response car to assist.

The final thing that decided it was a pursuit was when he drove straight through a set of red traffic lights at the junction with Nags Head Road (a notoriously dangerous junction). The chase was most certainly on, although not much of a contest with him driving a Rover and me an Allegro. My foot was hard down on the floor and the engine straining at top speed. As we approached Edmonton police station, I could see some distance ahead some of the lads from the station running out and throwing truncheons at the offending vehicle. They all missed him and thankfully me, trailing some distance behind. I managed to keep him in sight and after we took a few turnings ended up at the Cambridge roundabout at the junction with the A10 dual carriageway. He went the wrong way round this roundabout and then travelled North along the Southbound carriageway. After a mile or so he suddenly drove over the central reservation and then South along the Northbound dual carriageway after he saw another police car coming in the opposite direction, back towards the Cambridge roundabout.

By this time there were cars arriving from most of the North London areas and as he approached the roundabout there was a fast response car coming towards him. He decided to abandon his car whilst it was still moving and jumped over a railing fence into a large park. His car continued on driverless and ploughed into the oncoming police vehicle. Brian and I were out of our car and over the railings after him. In the park there could be seen numerous coppers running around asking if anyone had seen the suspect, which direction did he go and what was his description. After extensive searching there was no sign of the suspect so we decided to go back to the car and see what damage had been caused plus any clues as to the driver. As we walked back thoroughly dejected, a lady walking her dog asked us what was going on. When we told her we were looking for a suspect who had run off after crashing his car she said that she had seen a man hiding in a garden just along the road from where we were. We dashed off in the direction given after passing the information over the radio. A short distance away we came across a commotion in the front garden of a house and upon arrival observed several officers struggling on the ground with our suspect. Once subdued and handcuffed someone said, "Whose prisoner is this?" I said, "Mine." He was duly given over to my custody and was taken back to the local police station.

It turned out that he had, shortly before driving past our car, burgled a house and all the ill-gotten gains were on the back seat of the car. It was established that the car actually belonged to him. Some weeks later he came into the station to retrieve some of his property. He said that he would have had no problem if I had dished out some summary justice on the night he was arrested but that the cop that had, 'kicked him in the bollocks', whilst he was resisting arrest in the garden, was out of order. I'm sure that it must have happened accidently during the struggle!

Although I was not averse to driving fast, I like to believe that I did it without too much risk. However, that didn't seem to apply to some of my colleagues who were just nut cases. We were all sitting in the canteen one night playing cards when a call came over the radio that there was a man at someone's front door with a shotgun, threatening to shoot the occupant. We all scrambled out of the canteen, down the stairs and jumped into the nearest vehicle to set off to the scene. I had the misfortune to get into the passenger's side of a panda being driven by Ray. We screeched out of the back yard virtually on two wheels, narrowly avoiding oncoming traffic. After driving at great speed through junctions and red traffic lights we had gone about a mile when I said, "Stop the car." Ray said, "What's the matter?" I told him that I wasn't prepared to die on the way to an emergency call even if it involved a firearm, as we surely would if he carried on driving the way he was. I asked him to consider what might happen if we arrived screeching round the corner and skidding to a stop outside the address with the suspect still at the scene. Also, it would have taken several minutes from the time that police were called until it was relayed to the station. If the suspect was going to shoot someone, he would have done it before we might arrive on the scene and if not, he would be spooked into using the shotgun as we pulled up. We did continue to the scene at a more sedate pace and sure enough the suspect had fled the scene. It turned out to be a domestic dispute which we investigated and the suspect seen and dealt with later.

I did have my experience of being in a fast response car or as we called them, the area car. At this time, they were Mk II Rovers and covered a whole division or area, hence 'Area Car.' You had to be a class 1 driver to drive these and getting an advanced driving course was like gold dust so I had to be content with a posting as the radio operator. This meant answering radio calls from the control room at New Scotland yard on the car radio or from local stations over the personal radio system. You would be required to give a commentary if in a pursuit or give the driver directions to a scene or incident using the map. There was no such thing as a Satnav then, just good knowledge of your ground and an ability to follow and give directions whilst being flung about at high speed in the passenger seat, sometimes at night with the aid of a torch. The area cars were equipped with high-powered hand-held search lamps and a bullet proof clipboard. There were many exciting, frightening, funny and exhilarating incidents during my attachments during those years and I will relate just a few here.

One driver I was assigned to was having his first day back as an area car driver after having served a one-year ban following an accident he had been involved in as a police driver (this was common practice). We were just at the edge of our ground visiting a farm to pick up some eggs when a call came out on the main car radio to a robbery in Edmonton. It was a distance away but wouldn't take us long if we took the A10 dual carriageway and as we were right next to it at the time, decided to ask to be shown attending. Off we set at a fair rate of knots when we encountered a car in the outside lane up ahead. There was nothing in the inside lane so no reason for him to be in the outside lane and Bob, my driver, flashed his lights and lit up the blue flashing light on the roof. There was no response from the driver even after the loud two-tone claxon was sounded. He appeared to be having a deep and meaningful conversation with his front seat passenger.Bob, being mindful of his recently attained driver status, refused to overtake on the inside in case the driver suddenly pulled over. Other cars had already got to the scene of the robbery so we decided to give up and call in at Enfield Nick for a break.

We approached the traffic lights at the junction with Carterhatch Lane and as we did so the lights turned red for traffic travelling towards Edmonton. We were turning off to the right in a filter lane and now passing along the driver's side of the car who had not given way for us, so I wound down my window and shouted at the driver, "ARE YOU BLIND AS WELL AS DEAF?!" I think he was so shocked that he was distracted from the cars stopping in front of him at the traffic lights and whilst looking in my direction, crashed into the car in front of him. Bob got out of our car and was jumping on his hat whilst I got out and remonstrated with the offending driver. "I suggest that you pull over to the side of the road and exchange particulars with this man and think yourself lucky that we are not pursuing the matter." They were left to exchange details and we snuck off back to the station for our break. We never heard any more about this but Bob still laughs about it.

Most Nicks in the Met, or indeed anywhere, had activities that were particular to that station. Ponders Plonk was no different and we partic-ipated in several different types over the years. At first it was cards and the games of choice were, contract whist or hearts. It was whilst playing cards that I was first given the nick-name of, "Tricky Trayhorn". This stayed with me during my service and even to this day by some. We also had a period where darts was played every spare moment and then table tennis.

Chapter 11 – Family Life

These were happy years not only in my policing life but also married life. Since transferring into the Met and getting married my home life was amazing. Barbara and I organised our lives around my shift work and we spent quality time together with Kyri and Mark. We didn't have a lot of money to spend on fancy trips out or restaurants but were always doing something. Trips to the park, picnics, playing games, swimming and trips to the zoo or Knebworth. In October 1975 Barbara and I decided that we would try for a baby. To start with I wasn't sure but she said that she wanted one with me so it was in June of 1976 on the 11th that Stuart was born. I remember that it was a very hot summer that year and Barbara was in hospital for a few days prior to the birth.

I visited her after dropping Kyri and Mark at her Dad's house and then picked them up afterwards to take them home. I had just got them to bed one night when I got a call from the hospital. The nurse said, "Your wife has gone into labour and if you want to be here for the birth you'd better get here quickly." After a phone call to Barbara's Dad, he came to the house and I drove at top speed to the Hospital. When I arrived, I was dressed up in a gown and ushered straight into the delivery room. The Sister said, "I suppose you're used to this, being your third." I said, "Actually it's my first!" The Sister gave me a quizzical look and said no more. I held Barbara's hand whilst she had contractions and at one stage called me, "a bastard", I can't think why? At one point the Sister said, "You're frightening your husband Mrs Trayhorn." I'm not sure whether I looked frightened to her or whether I actually was? Anyway, Stuart came out very soon afterwards. We now had three children all of whom I adored and had great pleasure bringing up. Not that it was that easy – or cheap!

When I was on shift work I would either take them to school or pick them up depending on what shift I was on. Like many parents we were always running them backwards and forwards to football, rugby, swimming and cubs to name but a few. Apart from the usual difficulties that one encounters when children go through their teenage years, we had a good home family life. We were fortunate that none of them got into any trouble, or at least none that we ever became aware of. As I will relate later they have all turned out wonderfully and I am very proud of all of them.

Chapter 12 – Ponders Plonk – part two

So, back to Ponders End.

We were used to getting called to deal with some strange incidents and none so strange as one night in August 1977 when Brian (the Sergeant) and 'Carolyn actually' (the WPC) attended a call to a house in Brimsdown Avenue, Enfield Highway. Apparently, the children of the house had heard some strange knocking sounds coming from the walls and saw furniture moving on its own. The next-door neighbours had also witnessed the knocking and thought it frightening enough to call the police. I myself was dealing with another incident so never went to the house but Brian and 'Carolyn actually' talked to the rest of the relief back at the station about the incident. Both of them described the strange knocking sounds for which they could not determine the source. Carolyn, who was not given to fibbing, joking, exaggerating or making things up said that whilst Brian was upstairs, she saw a chair move three to four feet across the floor without any physical contact. She and Brian examined the chair closely and could find no strings, wires or any other means to explain the movement. The whole family and indeed, Brian and Carolyn were freaked out about this unexplained phenomenon. This incident became known worldwide as, "The Enfield Poltergeist." Books have been written about it as well as television plays and documentaries.

Back to a tour of duty on the Area car. Ron was the driver this time and noted for his fast driving skills when attending emergency incidents. He was fast and I was always hanging on for dear life when we were responding to such calls. One day we took a call to Edmonton and we sped out of the backyard of Ponders End police station at a high rate of knots. The roads were wet due to a light rain falling but this did not faze Ron. As we came round a slight bend approaching Edmonton Green, we came across stationary traffic at a set of red lights. There was a huge lorry in the inside lane and a row of cars in the outside lane. At the speed we were travelling there was no way we were going to stop in time and we slid for a good fifty yards avoiding the cars but going straight under the back of the lorry. The lorry had a low bar across the back known as a rear impact guard. Lucky for us, because as we disappeared into the bar, the front of the car dipped down and a shaving of metal, just like a woodworker's shaving of wood produced by a plane, rolled up from the front of the bonnet right up to the windscreen. We both got out of the car unscathed and to rapturous applause and much laughter from the crowds of people standing at the bus terminus on our left side.

To add insult to injury, a few days later we were minding our own business and making our way back to Enfield police station round the one-way system. We pulled away from a set of traffic lights which filtered traffic from a side road in to the main road. Traffic coming from the left, the only way it was allowed to come from, was stopped at a red light and so our light was green. No sooner had we pulled out than a car suddenly appeared from our right driving fast the wrong way down the one-way street and crashed into the side of our car. Needless to say the driver of that car was swiftly arrested. Being a stranger to the area and a bit lost, not being a suitable excuse!

On another shift with Ron on 27th November 1975 we were told to go to the Ridgeway in Enfield and form a road block at a specified junction. We had been informed that there had been a shooting at a house nearby and to stop any vehicles from entering the road. We found out later that the house belonged to Ross McWhirter and that he had been shot at his front door and taken to the nearby Chase Farm Hospital where he died shortly after being admitted. Together with his twin brother Norris, he was the co-compiler of the Guinness book of records. Ross had publicly offered a £50,000 reward for information leading to a conviction for several recent high-profile bombings in England that were openly claimed by the Provisional Irish Republican Army (IRA). The next night I sat in his kitchen together with Mick from our relief who was an authorised shot and had a firearm. We were house sitting just in case the killers returned. It turned out that the killers were Harry Duggan and Hugh Doherty who were two IRA volunteers. They were subsequently captured and charged with his murder and nine others. They were sentenced to life imprisonment but in 1999 they were released under the Good Friday Agreement. After a couple of nights, we resumed our normal patrols.

Another night and another driver, this time it was Chris. We got a call at about 2am to men fighting in the street with axes. It was winter time, freezing cold and with a smattering of snow on the ground. We made our way as quickly as possible to the scene of the reported fight and as we turned into the road, all was deadly quiet. Chris drove slowly down the road and we both had our windows wound down listening for any sounds of a disturbance. Suddenly Chris stopped the car and he was staring down onto the road out of his side window. I asked him what was up and he said that he thought he saw a leg in the road. He reversed up shining the car headlamps at the spot and we both got out to have a look. Sure enough, there in the middle of the road was a leg, it was a full-length leg in jeans and had a trainer on the foot. The top of the jean leg was covered in blood, which was also in the road around it.

We called back to the station what we had found and then fearing that there was a body lying nearby began a search of the surrounding area, looking in nearby alleys and over garden walls for a body. We found nothing and decided to return to the body part lying in the road, to protect the scene for any forensic evidence. Taking a closer look, we thought something wasn't quite right and gave the leg a poke with a foot. It turned out that it was in fact a false leg dressed up to look real and had tomato sauce smeared around the top to represent blood. We retrieved it and threw it into the boot of the car to show everyone at the station when we got back for our refreshment break. We discovered that it was a genuine false prosthetic leg but were unable to trace the original owner for who it must have been made. Whilst we were sitting in the station having our refreshments there was a phone call from somebody who through a fit of laughter told us that we had been fooled. So, it turned out to be someone's idea of a joke and we were indeed fooled. We never did find out who the prankster was. I can assure you that the leg looked pretty real when we first saw it.

There were many times that things happened that you least expect. Another incident that happened in the early hours of the morning was when I was out with Arthur, who was driving the panda around quiet and abandoned streets. The newspapers had been dropped outside a newsagent's shop tied up in bundles ready for when the shopkeeper turned up to open the shop. We observed two youths approach the bundles, rip one open and take out a newspaper and walk off with it. Arthur and I both thought he had a bloomin' cheek so decided to challenge them. One of the youths ran off and the other started to walk away quickly. He immediately became hostile towards us and so we pointed out that he was committing a theft. He said, "Alright I'll pay for it." I said, "It's a bit late to think about that now." He said, "Haven't you fucking bastards got anything better to do?" He took out some money from his pocket and threw it on the ground saying, "There's your fucking money." Arthur arrested him for theft stating, "Too late you're nicked." We got him into the back of the panda and I got in the back seat with him. Just as Arthur started to drive away the man started to struggle and behave aggressively. Arthur stopped and turned round to help and as he did so the man flung himself forward head-butting Arthur full in the face and loosening his front two teeth. When we got back to the station we were helped by other officers as he was still struggling. During the struggle he again lunged forward, this time engaging his forehead with my nose causing it to pour with blood.

The youth ended up being charged with theft and assault occasioning actual bodily harm. Arthur lost his front two teeth. At court the man's solicitor tried to plea bargain saying that he would plead guilty to theft if we dropped the assault charges. This was in the days before the Crown Prosecution Service dealt with prosecutions and we dealt with cases ourselves. Our response was a resounding," You must be joking mate." He was found guilty on both counts at Tottenham Magistrates court and fined a sum of money plus ordered to pay Arthur compensation for the loss of his teeth. I can't remember the amounts but there was a certain amount of justice meted out, although I don't suppose Arthur thought it was much consolation!

Arthur was a good mate and we spent a lot of time patrolling together. Arthur was driving one night on night duty and after a while driving round the quiet streets and factory estates, we decided to park up for a short time behind one factory to have a break. We both nodded off and the next thing I knew I was rudely awakened by several loud bangs and the panda car shuddering violently. I woke up immediately and saw that we had taken out a long stretch of wire fence at the side of the road. I believe that Arthur had woken prematurely and then drove off shortly to nod off again. Well I believe that is what might have happened but not the story told to the traffic Sergeant (which of course was the correct one!).

I told earlier of having dealt with mentally ill people and one of the worst I recall was when I was at Ponders plonk. A warrant had been issued under the Mental Health Act to remove a male named, to a mental hospital for assessment. There had been numerous complaints from neighbours as to his behaviour, saying to them that he could hear voices and they had observed that he always carried a large knife attached to his belt in a sheath. I turned up at the address together with Harry, a very large Sergeant and waiting outside was an ambulance. Harry knocked on the door and after a short time this rather large chap opened the door and I could straight away see a huge knife in a sheath attached to his belt. Harry reached out his hand as if to greet the chap with a friendly handshake, "Hello, my name is Harry." He said and gripped the chap's hand tightly, pulling him out of the doorway. I got behind him and before he had a chance and while Harry had hold of his hand so tightly, I managed to reach for the knife, pull it out of the sheath and throw it along the hallway.

The next thing we were all three of us rolling around on the floor. The ambulance guys came running over with a special stretcher, which we managed eventually to get him in and tied up so that he couldn't move. He was shouting out about being abducted by aliens and making weird noises. Because he was so strong and aggressive, I was designated to go in the ambulance to take him to the secure hospital whilst the Sergeant followed on behind. When we got to the hospital, we were directed through several locked doors arriving eventually to a padded cell where he was left on the stretcher to calm down and receive some form of medication. I was really glad to get out of that facility, it was a mad house!

I wrote earlier about, 'What goes round, comes round' and I have another story that illustrates this. I was on patrol one day in my panda when I was told to visit a building site where they had suffered a theft of a mobile generator. I attended and took full details to complete a crime report. I decided to do a few house-to-house enquiries to see if anyone nearby had seen anything. I drew a blank with this, apart from one lady who said that one evening she had seen a motorcycle and sidecar parked outside the building site. What was unusual about the sidecar was that it consisted of a black box instead of a fitting for a passenger to sit in. She said that there was an 'L' plate on the back of the box but she did not know the registration number, so there was no way of tracing it.

A few days later I was designated as Station Duty Officer, meaning that I was to deal with anybody coming into the station. Most of this duty revolved around, reporting accidents, giving advice re noisy neighbours, dealing with lost and found property, giving directions and checking driving documents as the result of the person having been given a 'producer'. One person came to the front counter and I noticed he had a crash helmet on. Looking out of the front window I saw that he had parked his motorcycle right outside on a yellow line. This didn't really bother me but his motorcycle happened to have a side car attached to it which was in the form of a black box with an 'L' plate on the back. He produced his documents to me and I said, "I think we have to talk about the mobile generator that you stole from a building site the other day." His face was a picture and without further ado he admitted that it was indeed he who had stolen the generator and was swiftly removed into the charge room. He had worked for a plant hire company and sold them the stolen generator for £200. Tottenham Magistrates fined him £200. The generator was recovered later and was returned to the owner.

If you had to attend court when you were on night duty, you were entitled to claim a minimum of four hours overtime plus travel time. This meant that it was worth while having an arrest that would ensure you got to court the next day. At that time when someone was arrested for a Breach of the Peace it was a requirement that the arresting officer appeared in court with the prisoner, who had to be brought before a magistrate as soon as possible. Could this be why there were so many people arrested for Breach of the Peace? If the Sergeant was in a good mood, he would let you go home around 02.00 if it was quiet and there were enough officers on duty. This meant you would get some sleep before attending court. When you got to court you would announce to the usher that you were off of night duty and then he would try and get your case before the magistrates as soon as possible. However, I'm not sure the ushers always believed you because officers would besiege them as soon as the court opened, saying they were off nights when they actually weren't. If you were unlucky you could be waiting until after lunch before your case was called.

Courts were sometimes pleasing, sometimes frustrating and sometimes amusing. Although not present myself, I heard of a traffic officer who arrested a youth for a public order offence. The allegation was that the youth had committed an offence of using abusive language in a public place. The magistrates wanted to know what was said. The traffic officer said, "I told him to move on and he told me to fuck off." The magistrates deliberated and decided that the officer should be used to such language and therefore they did not consider it to meet the criteria for the offence and dismissed the case. Later, the same officer appeared before the same magistrates with a motorist who he had reported for having a defective exhaust. He started to give a technical description regarding the exhaust system and escaping gas when the magistrate asked if the officer would explain in simpler terms. Without any hesitation the officer said, "Yes your worships, it had a fucking great hole in it."

The police family is made up of many interesting characters and some are quite eccentric. One such character was endearingly referred to as Paddy and yes, he was Irish. He didn't get involved much when it came to pro-active policing and I never knew him to have reported anyone for an offence or make an arrest. However, he always busied himself in the background, offered advice, collected bits of information, tidied up the tea room and made tea for the lads. He did not drive but had an old bike he used to ride around. When he was off duty, he used to ride around taking a note of which way the numbers ran of all the houses in a road. He noted these down on bits of paper and had dozens of them for streets all over the ground.

When a call came over the radio from the control room to attend a particular address, he would come onto the radio, "Unit attending the call to Alma Road, number 23 is as you turn in from the High Road the tenth house along on the left-hand side." This, although handy and useful information on occasions, did leave him open for ridicule. It became a game to get on the radio before Paddy with a description of where a particular house was. The next call that came out to an address one of us would get in before Paddy and in an Irish accent say something like, "Unit going to this call, if you enter the road from the High Street it is the fiftieth house on the right, the one with pink curtains in the window and roses growing round the front door."

That brings me to the saga of 'Paddy's rag'. He liked to clean up and make tea as already mentioned. He would ensure that the mugs were clean by using ajax scouring powder and a cloth. This cloth or rag was always in his hand and he would use it to clean the tables, the tea tray and the walls around the light switches. So, when he asked, "Do you want a cup of tea lads?" He would get a resounding, "No thanks Paddy!" The rag became a bit of a trophy and the game was to put it in places for someone to discover. It would turn up in the glove compartment of a panda, a lunch box, a locker and on one occasion was found flying from the flag pole on the roof of the station. I recall Barbara going to wash up my lunch box one day and saying, "What is this old bit of rag doing in your lunch box?" Good old Paddy, never ceased to give us cause for merriment.

In 1980 I was approached by a Sergeant (Joe) to become a tutor Constable, on a new scheme for training probationary constables. Apparently, this scheme was thought up by a woman Superintendent whilst she was ironing one day? At first, I declined this offer but Joe, the Sergeant, convinced me that it would be a good thing to be involved in. So, myself, along with another experienced Constable, Peter, became the division's 'Street Duty Course' trainers. Six probationers would be handed over to us for showing the ropes and guidance as to how things worked on the streets as opposed to the training school. We would arrange exercises for them like targeting trouble spots, dealing with traffic offences by stopping and checking vehicles and drivers and turning off the traffic lights at a junction so they got to practice doing traffic control.

One day I had booked out the divisional van to transport the probationers to different spots. I dropped off a couple at the Ponders End railway station with a view to catching people who were jumping over the fence after getting off a train, thereby dodging the paying of their fare. There was a perfect spot to observe at the back of a high-rise block of flats where you had a clear view of the station platform and the fence without being seen. I left the two probationers hiding at the back of the block of flats while I transported the rest to another location. Not too long after there was a radio call from one of the two probationers at the railway station asking for urgent assistance. I sped back to the flats to find one probationer sprawled on the ground and the other disappeared. I established that whilst they were peeking round the corner of the flats waiting for a train to arrive, the rear door to the flats burst open right next to where they were standing and two burglars came out carrying armfuls of stolen property. The probationers had wrestled with them but they had knocked them to the ground and ran off leaving a TV, video recorder, fur coat and items of jewellery scattered on the ground. One constable stayed, still stunned, on the ground and the other pursued the offenders. We and other officers began a search of the area including the underground garages of the blocks of flats nearby, that offered a good hiding place from pursuing police.

After a short time, the other probationer that had ran after the two burglars came back to where I was standing looking shocked and very pale. "Are you OK?" I asked. He replied, "I think I have just found a dead body." He took me to the underground garages and sure enough in one of the empty, derelict garages was a body. On examination I found that it was a male in his late teens and would appear to have died at least overnight as rigor mortis had set in. It was an intense learning experience for the new probationers and I told them that we had arranged everything that happened especially for them. The poor unfortunate teenager that passed away was found to have taken a drugs overdose and the coroner recorded a verdict of misadventure.

One of the probationers on a Street Duties Course came and asked me advice on an assault case he had been dealing with before coming on the course. He had not followed up on it quickly enough so I advised him what to do and assisted him. It ended up in a court case where the accused was pleading not guilty. Unfortunately, the probationer had not warned the witness in the case to attend the court date as instructed and the magistrates dismissed the case. This resulted in a complaint against the police for which I accepted responsibility.

After an investigation I ended up in front of the Chief Superintendent. He said, "I have read all the documents and reports relating to this complaint and I think that you have taken responsibility for this in a misguided attempt to dig the probationer out of the shit." I started to say something and he said, "I don't want you to say anything." He said that he had to give me words of advice and would record that he was giving serious consideration as to whether I was a fit person to run Street Duty Courses. He asked me if I liked running the courses and I said that I did. He said that he had no intention of taking me off this post and to be careful in the future. I carried on as usual and the probationer did not lose his job!

One set of recruits who was on one of our Street Duty Courses was Tim. I was showing him and the others on his course around the station on their first day and introducing them to the different departments. When I took them into the process section, I explained what they did and said that they must keep away from the young girl at one of the desks as it was my younger sister, Janine. At the end of the ten-week attachment to us, we arranged an end of course celebration at a local pub. One of the group approached me and said that Tim wondered if I would mind him asking Janine to the end of course do? I said, "First of all, it has nothing to do with me but if he thinks I am going to ask her for him he has another thing coming." He did ask her and now has been married to her for thirty-four years and they have three children and two grandchildren!

A lot of the new probationers had not seen a dead body so I would arrange a trip to the local mortuary. When scenes of a mortuary and a dead body are shown on television programmes, I have to say that it doesn't resemble any mortuary that I have visited. I have never seen just one table with a body on it and certainly none covered by a sheet! However, there was only the intention for the probationer to see a dead person before having to deal with one at the scene of an incident. I never intended that they should witness a full post mortem as this would not be necessary unless they progressed to the C.I.D. There may be occasions when an officer would be required to identify a body to a pathologist to ensure continuity for identification purposes. There was one mortuary assistant who would try and shock the probationers by producing a body part from a freezer or using his electric saw to remove the top off a skull whilst they were visiting. One of the most striking memories of a mortuary is the smell, something you never forget.

One of the worst things I found to deal with even more so than a dead body, was delivering a death message. How do you tell someone that their nearest and dearest has died unexpectedly and in tragic circumstances? There is no training I know of how to teach you this and no easy way to convey the information. I mention two occasions here purely to express the difficulty and truly emotional outpourings of grief. I was asked to call at one house to inform a wife that her husband had been involved in an accident and had suffered extremely serious injuries. When I knocked on the door a lady in her thirties opened the door and I asked if I could enter as I had some bad news. Obviously shocked, she invited me in. There was a dinner being cooked on the stove and a young child playing in the living room. "Sorry about the mess, we are just waiting for my husband to get back and I have been busy getting the dinner ready." I informed her of the accident and that she needed to contact the hospital to find out more about her husband's condition. As she was so shocked and visibly shaking, I phoned the hospital for her and managed to get through to the doctor dealing. He asked to speak to the wife and I put her on the phone. The doctor told her over the phone that her husband had passed away, she dropped the phone and gave an almighty scream. A close neighbour thankfully came to the house and once satisfied that I could do nothing more, I left the distraught woman to grieve and in the care of her neighbour.

On another occasion a call came through to call at an estate agent and tell a husband that his wife had died in a traffic accident and their 18-month-old baby was critically injured and not expected to live. As there were few details given, I first went back to the station to try and get more information before delivering such a message. I entered the estate agents and there was the usual banter and jokey comments from the staff. I remained solemn and asked to speak to the person named to me over the radio. He said, "OK it's a fair cop I'll come quietly." I asked if we could go somewhere private so we could talk and we went into a back office. I suspect by this time he realised that something was terribly wrong but nothing prepares you for that kind of bad news. There was no easy way to tell him so I just told him directly what had happened and that he needed to contact the hospital. After assisting with the call and ensuring that the staff at the shop were in support, I left. I know that the deceased person nor the family are known to me personally but delivering this type of message is draining and always left me feeling dreadful.

You don't expect people to thank you for breaking bad news to them but on occasions this can happen. I had to call round to one house to tell an elderly lady that her husband had collapsed and died in the street. The daughter of the elderly lady later sent the following letter: -

The Station Sergeant,

On Friday afternoon, the 22nd April my Father, (Name), collapsed and subsequently died in Southbury Road and my Mother wishes to thank the police officer who broke the news to her, and stayed until I could be contacted at work. Unfortunately, she was in no state to notice his number, but she was very touched by his concern. May I please also add my own thanks for his kindness shown to her in this terrible shock.

Sincerely (Name).

Sudden Deaths were fairly common and although most were due to natural causes we would mostly have to attend where a doctor was unable to issue a death certificate without the need for a post mortem examination. One of the phrases that was put in the report was always, 'I examined the body and could see no suspicious marks or scars.' So, in order to rule out foul play, even in the most innocent of cases, it was expected that you did just that. I had dealings with many deaths during my time as a constable, some were from old age and natural causes and some were due to accidents or suicide. The one thing I always will remember is dealing with the report that somebody had not been seen for some time and on approaching the address noticing hundreds of flies at the window and a distinct odour emanating through the letter box on the front door when looking inside. I will not go into details on any of these but will relate one that I particularly remember.

The son of an elderly lady who lived on her own reported by phone that he was unable to get an answer from his mother. I attended the bungalow and after getting no answer forced entry through the front door. I got no response to shouts of "Hello, anyone at home?" and started to look in the rooms leading from the hallway. When I entered the living room, I saw that it was in disarray with drawers pulled out and overturned on the floor, an ironing board tipped over and looking very much like the scene of a burglary. I continued my search, nobody in the kitchen and nobody in the bedroom and only one more room to check, the toilet. It was shut and apparently bolted from the inside. There was no response to knocking, so I forced it open to find the body of an elderly lady sprawled across the floor. She was semi-naked and looked very much like she had just got off the toilet. She had obviously been there for some time as when I checked more closely for signs of life, could tell that rigor mortis had set in.

Due to the state of the living room I radioed for the CID to attend as well as a Doctor to verify death. I stood at the door to wait their arrival and was surprised to see the duty Inspector turn up. I told him what I had discovered and he entered to see for himself even though I was trying to keep the scene free of disturbance to maximise any forensic evidence. He then decided that he needed to relieve himself and unbelievably stepped over the body, peed into the toilet, flushed it and then left. I thought, 'You'll never get a job as a detective!' and kicked myself for not being strong enough to say that he couldn't enter the scene until the Doctor and CID had attended. Lesson learned! The Doctor came and officially pronounced life extinct, the CID attended and agreed that it looked suspicious and unusually the coroner came to the scene. He made the decision that the death had been due to natural causes and ruled out any suspicious circumstances. So that was the end of that.

Ponders End was on "Y" division which also covers the Tottenham area. On Saturdays and sometimes on a Wednesday evening you could volunteer to do a duty at Tottenham Hotspur Football Club on home match days for overtime. Most of us would travel in our own cars or car sharing arriving at a preferred road for parking some half a mile from the football ground in White Hart Lane. It was difficult to get any nearer on match days due to the influx of supporters and the fact that there was a chance of the car being damaged on roads nearer to the ground.

The first port of call was to a local school where a hot meal would be provided for all police personnel. Next, we would parade outside the police room which was situated under the West Stand at 13.45 for a briefing. There would be rows of police lined up and an Inspector would call out everyone's name to ensure all were present. We would be given a card that indicated what your duty would be for that day. The Club only paid for a certain number of police inside the ground so the majority of us were given posts at roads leading up to the ground. Our job was to monitor crowds on their way to the match. Most fans were well behaved but there were always some who had been drinking and would be rowdy. I did witness on one occasion a visiting supporter's coach passing by one group and saw one of them throw something smashing the side window. I made my way towards him and on seeing me he ran off. I gave chase for some distance but with him being in lighter clothing than my full uniform, heavy overcoat and helmet, he fast disappeared into a nearby housing estate. When I got back to my post the coach had gone, presumably to the coach park. Come 15.00 there were only a few late stragglers still making their way to the ground and at 15.10 we had to report back to the police room for further instructions. As any action would be inside the ground during the match, we were allocated places in the stands, usually forming a thin blue line between home and visiting supporters.

I remember one match where we had to keep a whole section free from spectators in order to create a gap between home and visiting supporters. I'm convinced that there was a large element that were only concerned with getting at the opposing team supporters and not watch the football. On this occasion both sets of supporters vented their venom in our direction, shouting abuse, spitting and throwing coins with intent to cause injury. My colleague, Ned, wandered round picking up as many coins as he could and was hardly able to walk out at the end with pockets full of coins. Ten minutes before the final whistle we went back to our posts and remained there until the crowds had dispersed and everything calmed down. It wasn't always that easy however and when

Chelsea visited, their supporters tried to charge the home supporters in Park Lane. There were about a dozen or so of us in the middle with hundreds of rival supporters each side, intent at getting at each other. This is the moment that I became a great fan of the mounted police branch as they were at the junction of High Road and Park Lane, saw us halfway down Park Lane about to get trounced and came galloping towards us. Talk about being saved by the cavalry! We certainly were that day. Both sets of supporters ran off in all directions to get out of their way and we had thankfully been rescued. This was in April of 1975.

There was to be another even more frightening clash between Spurs and Chelsea in November of 1978, which I shall relate. But first I need to say what happened at the end of the match day. After the crowds had dispersed, we had to make our way back to the police room under the west stand to be checked off and hand our cards in. There were no smart rows now and as your name was called out you would shout "Here" and hand your card forwards for collection. There was one cheeky cop who would give his card to one of us earlier and would be on the bus travelling home early. (The same officer who had dragged the man out of his house after being told to fuck off during a domestic incident). When his name was called out a loud, "Here" would sound from the back of the gathered assembly of police and a card thrust forward. He was never found out.

Getting back to the Chelsea v Spurs incident. This time it was at Stamford Bridge and we were bussed to the ground to assist with the more unsocial and violent Spurs supporters. The atmosphere that day was explosive and it was obvious to the few of us in the stands that we were in trouble. I was with a few other police constables guarding a gate between the fence that separated rival supporters. The gate and fence were not to last for long and soon youths were clambering over the fence and breaking down the gate to get at their rivals. I managed to escape into the seated area above with hooligans trying to climb up after me. I was running backwards and forwards rapping the fingers of those trying to climb up with my truncheon. I think that it was the only time I can recall ever actually using my truncheon to strike anyone. I doubt that I broke any fingers and certainly never heard of any complaints. I can tell you that faced with so many aggressive and violent youths and men I certainly was fearing for my life. We thankfully survived the day without injury.

Not all football matches turned violent however and I did get to watch some of the game. The Wembley matches that I performed duty at were generally better humoured. It was the rugby cup final at Wembley that I remember mostly as the crowds that attended these events were much more friendly. I remember being assigned a post right at the top of one of the spectator stands and, on the way up, I had found a rosette of the team's supporters, dropped on the stairs. I attached it to my raincoat and was warmly greeted at the top by all the fans. A can of beer was thrust into my hand and an arm placed round my shoulder. I was adopted by the crowd and at the end not only had I done my duty in keeping order but was quite merry when I got on the coach to go home.

In 1976 The Notting Hill Carnival ended in a riot which prompted a heavy police presence from that year onwards. I remember attending each year and mostly being on stand-by at local schools. In order to stop us becoming bored they would set up the school hall as a cinema and play us films. I don't know who chose the films but I do recall that one of them was 'Zulu'! We would sometimes go on walks through the crowds in pairs. Thousands of people would be crammed into narrow streets with a loud sound system on every corner blasting out reggae music. During one walkabout I needed to use the little boys' room so popped into one of the schools being used as an operational H.Q. As I was on the way out, I walked round the corner of a corridor not paying attention and knocked into a chap coming the other way. "Sorry mate." I said. He just looked at me and walked on followed by several others. It was pointed out to me that the person I had nearly just knocked flying was the Commissioner, Sir Kenneth Newman. So, I can honestly say that I once bumped into the Commissioner of the Metropolitan Police.

Because of the number of pickpockets operating amongst the crowd as well as the groups of youths who would, 'steam' through stealing anything they could get their hands on, there were portacabins set up here and there as crime reporting stations. One year I was assigned to one of these together with a couple of colleagues. All was going well and we were recording numerous reports of theft and robbery when we suddenly came under attack from a bombardment of rocks and bricks. We had no choice but to abandon the portacabin and run for it. We commandeered dustbin lids from nearby properties in order to fend off flying bricks and stones being thrown at us by the mob. Notting Hill Carnival always seemed to end up in public disorder but provided me with plenty of overtime.

Between 1976 and 1978 we were to spend many visits to Dollis Hill in Willesden where was situated the film processing laboratories of 'Grunwicks'. Here there was a long running dispute between the mainly female, East African Asian workforce and management. Every day a bus load of workers, who were crossing the picket lines, would be descended upon by hordes of strikers and their supporters with the scenes becoming increasingly ugly. We would line the streets leading up to the factory gates and as the bus approached try to keep the hundreds of people out of the road. This dispute was shown nightly on the news, especially when the trade union movement as a whole got behind the dispute and the pickets started to number hundreds. As usual, the police were caught in the middle of these disputes (of which more later) and had to try and enforce the law.

One day in particular our contingent was dropped off by coach in the road leading up to the factory to await the daily crush when the pickets tried to stop the bus from entering the factory. The coach was parked at the side of the road together with a line of many others. Suddenly down the road came hundreds of pickets with banners and led by none other than Arthur Scargill. He stopped right next to our coach and began to give a speech about solidarity and the Miners Union support for the rights of the worker. Our coach driver started up his engine and pumped the accelerator making Arthur Scargill disappear in a big plume of exhaust fumes. It was a hilarious moment but whether it was ever shown on TV, I don't know. The one thing that any cop who was at any of those daily crushes will tell you they remember most, then it will be the dispensing by the mobile catering vans of frozen pork pies. I'm not sure if we were supposed to try eating them or throw them at the pickets?

In April 1981 we were again bussed en masse from all areas of the Met to assist local officers in Brixton where there had been rioting.

Trouble had been brewing here due to a police operation to try and reduce the high levels of crime in the area and a part of that operation was the use of stop and search powers. There had also been an incident where a black youth had been stabbed by other black youths and was being looked after by a police officer. A police car turned up to transport the wounded victim to hospital as a matter of urgency and a crowd of black youths, thinking that the police were arresting him, dragged him from the police car. Rumours spread that the wounded youth had been left to die by the police or that the police looked on as he was lying on the street. This had sparked an outcry from a large part of the African Caribbean community and led to hundreds of youths running riot. Again, we were deployed in large numbers to make arrests and keep order. I remember the streets around Railton Road looking like a battlefield. Bricks and debris lying everywhere and shops with broken windows. There were reports on the radio of petrol bombs being thrown but I never witnessed that myself.

It was a different story at Finsbury Park a few weeks later where an overspill of the Brixton troubles occurred on a bank holiday weekend fair. I, together with a contingent of my colleagues from Ponders End were on duty at what was supposed to be a fun family day with a fun-fair and bands playing in Finsbury Park. We were strolling around in pairs amongst the crowds with everyone in good spirits. As usual we found a good place to stand in the Seven Sisters Road outside a pram shop and opposite a Kentucky Fried Chicken. It was a good spot because we were offered to call round the back of the pram shop a couple at a time for a cup of tea.

All of a sudden, over the other side of the road a large group of youths entered the Kentucky Fried Chicken take away shop. There could be seen a lot of fighting and shouting before the window was smashed and the youths began to run out. I started to run across the road towards the scene when one of the cops with me held me back and said, "Hang on there are not enough of us to deal with that lot, wait until help arrives." Within minutes there was a large contingent of officers with shields spread across the road. The youths, of which there were dozens by this time ran off along Seven Sisters Road. Every car and bus that came along the road past the mob had their windows smashed and as we chased them, I could see that they had smashed the windows of the houses and hotels also. Some had tried to set fire to the curtains hanging in the smashed windows, without success. The Commander, who had been standing nearby was struck on the head with a brick. I rated this as one of the most frightening riot situations that I witnessed taking place right in front of me. My colleague had been right to pull me back but it makes me so mad to see mob violence going unchallenged or unpunished. It was always very frustrating.

Just to prove that I didn't spend all of my time at the scenes of riots, disputes and public disorder, I can relate my experience of a more pleasant assignment. In 1982 Pope John Paul II visited Britain over three days at the end of May. During the times that he was in London we were deployed along the routes of his processions through the streets to ensure his security. I'm not religious myself and especially not of the Roman Catholic persuasion. However, there was an overwhelming outpouring of adoration from thousands of people and a genuine concern that his well-being and safety might be at risk. Together with hundreds of other police personnel, I stood at the kerb of a road on his route facing the crowd. Our job was to watch the crowd and get to know who was in the section in front of us, to identify anyone who might be a risk. The Popemobile passed by with much shouting, cheering and hysteria. The next day I was stationed inside Wembley Stadium where the Pope was to take Mass. The stadium was as packed as any football extravaganza and just as euphoric in its nature. Again, our brief was to adopt a section of the crowd and spot anyone who was acting strangely. On this occasion I was drawn to a man a few rows back from the front who was highly excitable and, in my opinion, acting very strangely. I reported this to a supervising officer and a short time later a couple of plain clothed officers escorted the man away in order to check him out. I never heard what happened to him but I suspect that he was just a very excitable guy freaked out at seeing his idol. I very much came to love the Pope because I earned a lot of overtime from his visit, oh and of course brought much happiness to the Roman Catholic population of London!

Other events that I attended in London in the early 80's were, Trooping the Colour, which is to celebrate the Queen's official birthday, state openings of parliament, state visits (Sultan of Oman, His Majesty Qaboos Bin Said Al Said, the Queen of the Netherlands and Prince Claus) to name but a few. There were also the regular marches and demonstrations during the summer months mainly and I referred to this period as the silly season. The Gay Pride march was always very good natured, although I have to admit that I never really got used to seeing two men dressed in next to nothing, openly cuddling and kissing each other. The contrast between the participants and the police escorting them was quite marked. I remember being at one protest march for the Campaign for Nuclear Disarmament (CND) in 1984 and getting the feeling that the participants all seemed of a certain type. My stereotypical mentality was reinforced when, at the end of the march I heard a group say, "If we're quick we can just get to the Embankment in time to join the protest march starting from there." So much for their commitment to a particular cause! The term 'anarchist' springs to mind.

In amongst all the demonstrations, riots and public order events there were still the everyday patrols and calls to deal with. On 25th September 1983 I was on night duty when we were called to suspects on premises. How do I know the date? Because it is in my diary from that year that I had a Tetanus Booster on that date. Why did I have a tetanus booster? Because when we reached the premises where suspects had been seen and started searching the area, we disturbed a burglar at the rear of a house. A chase quickly ensued and I was jumping over garden fences in hot pursuit of a darkly clad male suspect. I don't know if you have seen the film, 'Hot Fuzz', where the cops are leaping over fences in pursuit of a suspect? Well it was along those lines. I was a bit like the one that smashes through the fence only with me, I jumped over one fence and landed on a piece of broken fence with a nail sticking up. I landed heavily and the nail went straight through my boot and into my foot. I now had a large piece of fence attached to my foot so my chances of catching the suspect were now out the window. The suspect was caught but I was off to hospital for my tetanus booster after prising the plank and nail from my foot.

Around this time there was a severe overcrowding of prisons and in order to cope with numbers, some police stations were used as temporary prisons. The cells were not really suitable for long term residents but were used for some time. Police officers were used as gaolers and all on overtime! I never experienced any problems with the prisoners at Cheshunt. Most were amicable, although none who you would want living next door to you! They were the neediest group of people you could imagine and the amount of prescription medication kept for them was enough to stock a small chemist shop.

Chapter 13 – Sergeant Trayhorn at Holloway

I had tried on three occasions to pass the Sergeants exam, mainly because at each year's appraisal the Inspector would encourage you to put an application in to take it. I never really took it that seriously until 1982 when I attended pre-promotion classes and studied hard. Unfortunately, I did not pass again so decided not to bother anymore and remain as a Constable driving my panda and the divisional van as well as acting as radio operator in the area car. I was in the station one day in late 1983 when the Chief Superintendent came in. When he saw me, he said, "You're sitting the Sergeant's exam this coming year." I said, "No sir I've decided not to bother this time." He said, "That wasn't a question, you ARE sitting the exam and I expect to see your application on my desk." That was probably the push that I needed.

The style of exam at that time was very much having to remember great chunks of operational orders as well as knowing legislation and procedure. I would take the reference books out with me in the panda and on early turn I would buy a packet of dry roasted peanuts and sit up quietly somewhere, eat the peanuts whilst reading and reciting chunks of information. Repetition, repetition, repetition, the same principal as learning lines for plays, as I found out later. So it was that I sat the exam and whilst out and about in my panda patrolling on night duty one night in March 1984, I was called to the station by the Inspector who said, "I have spoken to a contact at the Yard and he tells me that you passed the exam, congratulations Sergeant Trayhorn." I was a bit in shock and not sure whether to believe him, however, it was confirmed in Police Orders on 27th March. I had been a Constable for fourteen years did not consider myself Sergeant material but now there was no going back. The next day I had a hand written note of congratulations from a Superintendent at Scotland Yard:

Dear Malcolm

Congratulations, I was very pleased to see your name in the list of those who have passed the exam. I hope you believe all the work was worthwhile.

Having worked briefly with you several years ago I believe that you will be a good P.S. and perhaps we will serve together again in the future

Well done, Best Wishes

Tony (name – a former chief inspector at Enfield)

I also received a memo from the Chief Superintendent who had insisted I took the exam: -

I was delighted to read police orders of last night and there to learn of your success in the promotion exam.

I regret I am unable to see you due to your being annual leave but would wish to take this opportunity of offering my most sincere congratulations. (Name) Chief Superintendent.

I was actually quite shocked to learn that I had at last succeeded. I always tell people that I had saved up 25 Kellogg's Cornflake packet tops and sent them off with a postal order for seven and sixpence in order for them to send me back my stripes! I thought that I had plenty of time to get used to the idea as it usually took several months before there was a place on a Sergeant's promotion course at Hendon. This was not the case, however and in a very short period of time I was informed that I was to attend a pre promotion course at Hendon on the 8th May and promoted on 4th June. During the course my fellow course members and I were given our respective postings, mine was to 'N' Division Holloway. "And good luck to you mate!" was a comment made by my classmates and I was wondering what I'd let myself in for?

I was soon to find out and on 4th June I paraded in front of the Commander of 'N' division at Kings Cross police station to be welcomed to the area. Holloway police station was situated in Hornsey Road and totally different from Ponders End in every way. There were eight Sergeants and twenty P.C.s on each relief with an Inspector in overall charge. This was only on paper, however and as was the case at Ponders End, that number was rarely paraded. I was shown round the ground by one of the other Sergeants but I have to say that I never really got to know it and was always a bit disoriented and lost. This was demonstrated when I was delegated to drive the Inspector around the ground together with another Sergeant. The Inspector had his own Duty Officers unmarked car but he always expected to be chauffeured around by a Sergeant. I think that this was because he wanted to ensure that he wouldn't actually be expected to do any police work. Anyway, after some time driving around, he said, "Right make your way back to the station without us directing you." I drove round desperately trying to find somewhere that looked vaguely familiar or might give me a clue as to where I was but was totally lost. After what seemed an age the other Sergeant said, "We'd better tell him as we are now miles off our ground."

I found that a lot of a Sergeant's time was spent in the station either as station officer and subsequently as Custody Sergeant. I found this alien to what I was used to and probably still had a PC's mentality. This was demonstrated when I was again chauffeuring Brucie, the Inspector, around one day. A call came out on the radio to a disturbance on a street near to where we were so I answered up that we were attending. Brucie looked daggers at me and said, "What the hell are you doing?" I said, "We're nearest so I thought we could take it." We turned the corner and there in front of us were two men fighting. I got out to separate them and was suddenly rolling around on the ground with Brucie grappling with the other man. My specs went flying and I was conscious that they were in the road and at serious risk of being crushed under foot in the ensuing brawl. Once the troops arrived and things settled down, I retrieved my unscathed specs from the middle of the road. We got back in the car and Brucie told me in no uncertain terms that as a Sergeant I was not to answer calls as I was now a Supervisor. I never really got used to this concept, I suppose as I had been a PC for 14 years I was used to answering and dealing with incidents.

I remember vividly my first day in charge of Highbury Vale police station, which was a sub divisional station to Holloway. I was getting familiar with the station and suddenly the rear door from the back yard into the charge room burst open and a male came flying in closely followed by two officers. He looked to have been dragged through a hedge backwards. I can't remember what he had been arrested for but a short time later a similar entrance through the back door drew me to the conclusion that the way of dealing with things was different than I was used to.

I was the Custody Officer in July 1984 during a night duty and was responsible for those being kept overnight in the cells. Apart from dealing with new prisoners coming into the station I was responsible for checking those already in cells, especially the drunks. There was one elderly man who had been arrested for highway obstruction and due to appear at court the next morning. I ended my shift at 06.00 and handed over all prisoners to the early turn Custody Sergeant. I did a final check on the prisoners together with the incoming Sergeant before leaving for home. Later that day I was called back to the station where it had been found that the elderly man had died before being taken from the cell to be transported to court. Thankfully I had dealt with him correctly and it was subsequently established that he had died during the morning from natural causes. It just taught me that however busy you are and how obnoxious people are, you have a duty of care and must make sure that they are treated properly.

1984 was the year that the Police and Criminal Act came into force, which meant huge changes to the way things should be done. A Sergeant was now designated as a Custody Officer with sole responsibility for prisoners and the charge room instead of looking after the station office as well. Holloway custody area was a very busy place and during any shift, day or night, it would be heaving with prisoners. There were three cell passages with a total of about 10 cells plus two detention rooms. It would not be unusual for most of these to be full at the busiest times and there would be two Sergeants on the go for the whole shift just trying to keep up with the volume of work. Everything you could imagine came in through the back door, drunks, drug possession, drug searches, thieves, shop lifters, burglars, drink drivers, prostitutes, TWOC'ers (Taking Without Consent), Breach of the Peace, criminal damage, assaults and people with a mental problem, to name but a few.

Most of the offences tended to revolve around drink or drugs so a lot of the people that came through the door into the charge room were either off their heads or aggressive and difficult to deal with. Prostitutes would usually be friendly as they were looking to get back out on the streets as soon as they could, to get on with business. I have to say that all of the 'ladies' that came in front of me I wouldn't describe as attractive nor would I want to have any form of liaison with them even if they were the ones paying me! I remember a regular whose name was Heather. She was brought before me one afternoon, "Hello again Heather, turn out your pockets and handbag so I can list your property." She did so and from her handbag she produced six unused condoms and four pence cash. I said, "Oh I see you have only had four customers today Heather." She replied, "You cheeky bastard."

We had a regular drunk whose name escapes me but who could forget a one-legged drunk? When giving evidence in court for the offence of being drunk it was nearly always, "His eyes were glazed, his speech was slurred and he was unsteady on his feet." I always wondered what an arresting Constable giving evidence would say? Probably, "And he was unsteady on his foot your worships!" or, "He was legless your Worships!"

In May of 1985 I booked in a prisoner who had been arrested for being in breach of his conditions to enter the U.K. He was a particularly difficult person to deal with and ended up being at the station for some time whilst his status was established. He was also searched and found to be in possession of a quantity of cannabis. He subsequently made a complaint that he had been unlawfully arrested and kept in custody too long. Other Sergeants were involved at different times during his time in custody and we were all subject to investigation. This went on for some time and didn't finish until June of 1988. Eventually, he was found to have been working in breach of his landing conditions and following advice from his counsel decided to drop his complaint against the Commissioner.

One male prisoner came in to the custody area and was totally uncooperative and argumentative so was placed directly into a cell having his laces and belt removed, as was common practice. The next thing he did was to remove his shirt, roll it up and try and strangle himself with it. This was taken from him as were his trousers, which he did the same thing with. It ended up with him being stark naked in the cell and we also had to remove the mattress when he started tearing off strips to make a ligature. Having no way to try and strangle himself he started running as fast as he could across the cell and head butting the wall. The Doctor had been called and ended up issuing a Mental Health Act order after a second opinion was obtained.

One night, quite late, a Constable brought in front of me a man who was reported to have been driving erratically but the street breath test had proved negative. I put him on the evidential breath machine that was kept in a small room behind the charging desk and that came back negative as well. The man was obviously under the influence of something and didn't look great so I called for an ambulance. He was taken to hospital where they found that he had taken a near fatal dose of Mogadon tablets. Another case where duty of care came before administering justice.

On another occasion a man was brought in for having produced a positive breath test on the street after an accident. I had a strict procedure to follow at the station and everything was read out from a booklet that was an idiot's guide to follow. Firstly, I required him to provide two specimens of breath on the evidential breath machine. This machine was specially calibrated and would give readouts at each stage of the process. Firstly, it gave a zero reading, then a calibration check from a known sample in a bottle next to the machine, then a zero reading before the suspect gave a first sample of breath. Next another zero reading after the machine had purged the previous one, then a second sample from the suspect and then a zero reading before a final calibration check and a final zero reading.

Quite often people would pretend to blow or suck in a vain attempt to claim that it wasn't working, however there was no way to fool the machine. This person was compliant and blew two samples which both gave a reading over the legal limit. However, the final calibration reading came back as 'Low – Abort', which meant I couldn't use either of the readings. I now had to go to the second phase which was to demand blood. Although not happy about this he agreed so I called out the Doctor from a list kept in the custody suite. This was a local Doctor who attended after half an hour or so. The Doctor that turned up was an Irish man who had just slung on a pair of tracksuit pants and a sloppy joe jumper. He didn't look much like a Doctor and this was immediately commented on by the suspect. We entered the Divisional Surgeon's room and the Doctor asked the man to roll up his left sleeve whilst he prepared his hypodermic syringe and tubes. After swabbing the inside of his arm, the Doctor proceeded to, what I can only describe as, stab the man with the syringe and move it around this way and that whilst he tried to extract some blood. After not being successful he pulled the needle out and then stabbed him again in the attempt to find a more successful spot.

By this time the suspect was voicing his objections and querying if the person in front of him was really a Doctor. Two plasters were now stuck on his arm to cover the puncture wounds and the sleeve on his right arm rolled up. Another unsuccessful stab later the Doctor said, "Sorry Sergeant but I can't get any blood out of this man." I was tempted to say, "That's because his name is Stone" but I didn't. The man was brought back in front of my desk and I said that we would now move on to the third phase and the man said, "Now you're taking the piss." I said, "It's funny you should say that, I now require two specimens of urine within an hour." He did in the end and after being analysed, the reading eventually came back that he was over the legal limit. I must admit that I felt sorry for him really, he had gone through enough punishment already!

Although it sounds as if I was in the custody suite constantly, I actually did manage to get out now and again. Whilst out in the Duty Officer's car one day, without Brucie, I took a call to an elderly woman not seen for over a week, as all the lads were busy on other calls. It was a first floor flat with a door and kitchen window facing to the front. There was no answer to repeated knocking and looking through the letter box I could see that the door was barricaded from the inside with pieces of furniture. There was a tell-tale smell coming from inside so I knew what I was going to find when I got in!

The only way in was to smash the kitchen window, so out came the truncheon and after clearing a large enough hole to crawl through I gingerly made my way inside. Lo and behold on the bedroom floor, face down, was the lifeless body of an elderly woman. I called for a Police

Doctor to come and pronounce life extinct as I was not qualified to do so, even though it was obvious that she had been dead for some time. As the Doctor was coming, I removed the barricade from the front door but couldn't find the key to unlock it. I searched high and low and thought it must be on her body so I turned her over to see if it might be hanging round her neck or in her pocket. This was a big mistake as the flies and maggots had been doing their job. I won't describe the sight or smell any further but I can assure you it was not pleasant. There was a knock on the door and it was the Doctor. I spoke to him through the kitchen window telling him that the door was locked with no sign of a key and he would have to climb through the window as I had done. "There's no chance of me climbing through there," came the reply. So, I had to climb back out of the broken window and smash down the front door from the outside. The Doctor confirmed that the woman was dead ("No shit Sherlock!") so I called the undertakers and secured the scene. I had to have that uniform thoroughly cleaned to get rid of the smell but had to throw the rest of my clothes, including underwear, away.

Another time I was on my own early one morning I took a call to the Arsenal underground station to a man under a train. I knew that the transport police would deal with this incident but attended the scene anyway. When I got there, I went down onto the platform where a train was standing but could find no trace of any train staff or anybody else. I walked to the front of the train where I found the driver sitting in his cab. I said, "We received a call that someone had been run over by a train?" He quite calmly said, "Oh yes he's under the train alright." I took my torch and walked along the platform looking through the narrow gap onto the track. About halfway down I saw a face with eyes wide open staring back at me. The Transport Police arrived shortly after this and one of them crawled under the train from the end (the power had been turned off). Upon reaching the body he made sure that he was clear of the rails and came back out so the power could be switched back on and the train moved forward clearing the body. It was then lifted up onto the platform to be dealt with. Fortunately, it was in one piece. It turned out that the man was on his way home from work as a Chef and had committed suicide by jumping in front of the train.

In 1984 the Miners' strike began and continued for a whole year. Each week a contingent would leave from all over the Metropolitan Police area to bolster the Northern forces and effectively help Margaret Thatcher's government to break the strike. There were ugly scenes and many clashes as pickets tried to stop those still working from going to work at the mines still open. Coaches were hired to take police to trouble spots and each one contained one Inspector, two Sergeants and twenty P.C.s. I was detailed on one of these trips and was billeted for a week at an army camp in Nottinghamshire. When we first arrived, we were invited to have a meal in the Naffi (Navy Army & Air Force Institutes) canteen. However, when I went to enter with the lads the person on the door saw my stripes. I was stopped and politely told that I had to dine separately from them in the Sergeant's mess. Well, I couldn't believe the attention I received with soldiers calling me sir and attending to my every whim. The food was excellent and as I found out of far superior standard and choice than that dished out to the lads. I thought, where do I join up!

We were taken from there each day to Billsthorpe Colliery to facilitate entry into the colliery by those still working. We lined the road on both sides holding back the pickets as they shouted abuse at the bus load of workers going past. The pickets we dealt with were not as militant as in some other areas and we would stand around chatting with them before and after the coaches went past. We used to get rations of food supplied to us at the army camp and decided that we would give these to the retired miners who would attend their canteen each day. We built up such a good rapport with all at Billsthorpe that we would get invited into their canteen in the mornings for a good old fry-up breakfast and a big mug of tea. On the wall of the canteen was a display cabinet which had police uniform epaulettes from various police units that had been on duty at the pit. Mine was one that was included in the collection so N92 was probably displayed there until the pit closed down in 1997. We were also invited on a trip down the mine to see for ourselves the working conditions of the miners. On 15th November 1984, we descended down the main shaft to a long tunnel which we went along crouching down until we reached the coal face. It was a great visit and we left with a certificate signed by the colliery manager to say that we had descended the shaft. We were also presented with our own miners' helmet, a lamp check token stamped with our shoulder number, a mining colliery deputy's yard stick and a national union of miner's lapel badge. On top of all that the overtime for that week paid for bikes for Kyri, Mark and Stuart that Christmas. I was humbled by the kind treatment and friendliness of the miners we met and a little bit ashamed that we as the police were effectively used by the government at the time to break the miners and devastate the mining industry and communities, rightly or wrongly.

In February 1985 I went to premises in Holloway to support PC's who were attending a difficult eviction by bailiffs from Clerkenwell County Court. The woman occupant was shouting and screaming and being particularly obstructive and uncooperative. I spent some considerable time explaining that she had to leave in accordance with the warrant and the bailiff's instructions. As she was not listening and becoming more threatening, I suggested that the bailiffs remove her forcibly from the premises whilst we remained in support. They managed, with a struggle to eject her from the premises and fortunately we did not have to arrest the woman.

Subsequently a letter of thanks arrived from the court: -

Thank you for the assistance of Sgt N92 Trayhorn and several P.C's given to my two bailiffs on Monday the 11th February 1985. With the help of your officers, in particular Sgt Trayhorn, we were able, after some consider-able time, to evict a very difficult occupant by my two bailiffs carrying her from the premises. Please convey our appreciation to the officers concerned for their support. (Signature) Supervising Bailiff

I was getting used to the roll of Sergeant, although I did really see myself as one of the lads. When going for a drink in the pub after duty the lads used to say, "Here he comes, Malcolm, don't call me Sergeant, Trayhorn." A new Sergeant was under a probationary period of a year and you were unable to apply for any specialist rolls until after that period had passed and you were confirmed by the Commander. A few months into my probationary period I was approached by the duties Sergeant who said, "You used to be involved with the Street Duties

Training courses at your last station didn't you?" I confirmed that I was and he asked if I would be interested in running them at Holloway. I said that I couldn't apply as I was still a probationary Sergeant. "Don't worry about that, are you interested?" I certainly was and so I was now in charge of Street Duty Courses at Holloway, probably because no one else was interested. However, this was a good move for me as it got me out of Custody Office duties for ten weeks at a time whilst the course was running. Ten new recruits would be assigned to me at a time and I had two experienced PC's to help me. I would assign each officer a beat to cover and send them out to gather information, speak to the public, report motorists for traffic offences and make arrests. I and the two experienced officers would meet up with them during their patrols and walk with them.

The Chief Inspector Operations would ask me to deal with issues that had been complained about when he had attended community meetings so he was always happy with us. There was a portacabin in the yard at Holloway at this time as the front counter area was being renovated. I was sitting in there one day when one of the young new probationers came in looking very flushed and upset. "And what's the matter with you?" I said. He replied, "I've just had the piss ripped out of me Sergeant." When I asked him what the problem was, he said that he had arrested someone for being drunk and had taken the prisoner into the charge room through the back door. The Custody Sergeant had apparently promptly thrown him and the drunk prisoner straight back out the door into the back yard. I said, "Where is the prisoner now?" He said, "Outside the portacabin Sergeant." I looked outside the door and sure enough there was a very drunk man leaning up against the outside of the portacabin. "Right wait there I'll soon sort this out." I said and went inside to challenge the Custody Sergeant for refusing my probationers sound arrest. He was up to his eyes in prisoners and had a queue waiting to be booked in and said, "Malcolm, look at this lot, I've got every cell doubled up and nowhere to put new prisoners, I thought I would clear out some of the less important ones such as the drunks so I kicked one out of the front door, five minutes later your young lad brings him back through the rear door." I booked out the divisional van, got the drunk and the probationer in the back and gave the man a lift home to prevent him being arrested further that day.

In June 1985 I was attending a course at Hendon Training School which was due to last a week. My transport at this time was a Honda 90c.c. motorbike and as I was making my way home on Tuesday 25th June, I was knocked off by a car that turned right, across my path sent me sprawling across the road. I knew at once that I had a serious injury to my right leg which had been torn open as I sailed across the tarmac and stony road surface. I was conveyed to Barnet Hospital where the casualty doctor and nurse cleaned up the wound, taking out all the loose road gravel and dirt that had got in whilst I slid across the road. They poured some sort of liquid into the wound which fizzed up lifting out lots of dirt and small stones. After making sure that it was clean of foreign material, they set about closing up the wound, which looked a bit like a jigsaw puzzle.

It took 13 stitches to close the wound after which it was heavily bandaged and I was seated in a wheelchair with my leg up awaiting the arrival of Barbara to pick me up. When the car eventually pulled up outside the casualty department, I had been waiting such a long time that I was just wanting to get home. As I was manoeuvred into the front seat, Barbara noticed blood seeping out of the bandage and thought that someone should take a look at it. I told her to leave it and let's just get home it will be fine. However, more blood seemed to be oozing through the bandage and dripping onto the car floor. Barbara went in to see the casualty staff and one of the nurses came out to take a look. I was promptly taken back into a room in the casualty area where the bandage was removed revealing a steady stream of blood seeping through the stitched-up wound. I was standing up when they cut two of the stitches and allowed a great gush of blood to flow. At this point I must have lost a fair amount of blood as the next thing I know I am sitting in the chair with people rushing round and the on-duty consultant called. I have a feeling that the staff who had seen me and dealt with me originally must have been reprimanded for missing that an artery had been cut. Had I gone home without being properly treated I could have bled to death. So, another brush with death averted!

They now treated the injury as it should have been dealt with in the first place and then I was admitted onto a ward so that my condition could be monitored. I had a large hole in the lower part of my right leg and it was found that I had two damaged ligaments. After a week it was decided that the leg had settled down sufficiently to have a plaster cast put on it. I was not allowed out of bed at this time and a hole had to be cut in the plaster to allow access to the hole in the leg for cleaning and dressing. After a week and a half, I was able to get out of bed and move around in a wheelchair as long as the leg was kept up. The Doctor dealing with me then examined the plaster and said that it would have to come off, the wound re-dressed and another plaster put on. I had visits from some of the lads from my relief at Holloway and made friends with others in the same ward as me. There was a hospital radio to listen to whilst relegated to the bed and someone would come round to ask for requests. I was listening one day and they played a classical piece that I thought was fabulous and asked for it myself. It was, 'Polonaise in a-flat major op. 53'. The cheeky chap in the next bed to me asked the nurse if they put bromide in the tea as he hadn't had a stirring in his nether regions since being in the hospital and with all the lovely young nurses tending to him then he should have felt something? She said that they certainly didn't and it was just that being in hospital meant that the mind was not focussed on such things. I think he was just trying it on, although I have to say that I hadn't experienced any carnal desires either. With little to do but lie in bed I put together one of my fabled odes: -

Ode to the Nurse by Malcolm Trayhorn 1985

I sit here on my lazy arse, watching all the nurses pass.
Busy in their daily tasks, doing all that anyone asks.
At six o'clock the day it starts, to the sound of coughs and spits and farts.
Yes, the sounds of the day begin at six, with drugs prescribed for my daily fix.
We all wait for the paper man, whilst nurse is dealing with another bed pan.
From the patients that they would like to throttle,
To the emptying of the dreaded bottle.
The food has made me gain a stone, "Nurse!" could you please pass the phone.
I'll need a leak that's for certain, and who is there to pull the curtain?

Yes, the nurse always comes to my aid, they are over worked and under paid.

So many jobs they have to fulfil, I hope they bring me another pill.

They'll change your dressing, wash your back, replace your bottle in its rack.

Give you tea and give you dinner, we all agree that each one's a winner.

They'll take your pulse and your blood pressure,

If you need some help, they'll even dress yer.

All these things and millions more, make the nurse a marvel of that I'm sure.

On the Friday of that week, and because they liked to clear out patients before a weekend, the doctor said that another hole needed to be cut in the plaster after which I could be released with crutches. I took eight weeks to recover sufficiently to return to work with several visits to the doctors for the wound to be dressed and extensive physiotherapy. The ligament damage is permanent but with regular exercise I managed fairly well. The one thing that I was advised against was playing squash, which I had really enjoyed up until the accident. I have not played it since and try to avoid any activity requiring sudden twisting and turning. I certainly know about it if I go too far with some activities. I never did forgive the driver of that car, who was proved to be the guilty party, even though she denied guilt right up until the day it was due to be heard by the courts. On the eve of the court date her solicitors offered an out-of-court settlement, which was accepted. The compensation I received paid for my daughters first wedding.

On 6th October 1985 there was a serious disturbance at Broadwater Farm in Tottenham. The events of the day were dominated by two deaths. The first was that of Cynthia Jarrett, an African-Caribbean woman who died the previous day owing to heart failure during a police search at her home. The second was the tension between the local black youth and the largely white Metropolitan Police that was already high due to a combination of local issues and the aftermath of another riot which had occurred in the Brixton area of London the previous week following the shooting of a black woman (Dorothy 'Cherry' Groce) during another police search. There was a demonstration outside Tottenham police station by a crowd of people. Violence between police and youths escalated during the day. Police in riot gear tried to clear streets using baton charges, whilst youths threw bricks and Molotov cocktails. At 9.30pm police and London fire brigade were called to Tangmere House to deal with a fire. The location itself was some distance away from the main body of rioting, and as such was being policed by units who were less well-equipped and not riot trained. As with most police operations at that time a number of officers would form a unit to work together (1 sergeant and 10 PC's), they were numbered and called 'serials'. The London Fire Brigade came under attack as did 'serial 502', who were designated to assist and protect them. They were overwhelmed and hastily withdrew, chased by a group of between 30 to 50 rioters. One of the police officers, P.C. Keith Blakelock tripped and fell. He was surrounded by a mob with machetes, knives and other weapons. They attacked him inflicting him with over 40 injuries and stuck a 6" knife in his neck. Other officers bravely rescued Richard Coombes, also under attack by the mob, and then returned to drag Keith to safety. Keith unfortunately died on the way to hospital. He was the first officer since 1833 to be killed during a riot.

This was happening just under four miles along the road from Holloway and we could hear events unfolding on the radio. Together with others I was despatched to the nearby Whittington hospital to guard Richard Coombes and other injured officers who were still receiving treatment, as well as some of the rioters. I remember vividly standing beside Richard's hospital bed and seeing the terrible injuries that he had received.

The next night there were rumours that youths on the Andover Estate at the rear of Holloway police station had stock piled petrol bombs in the underground garages in readiness for disorder and attack on the police station. Although not a rabbit warren of buildings like the Broadwater Farm estate, there were lots of social housing properties all closely packed into a small area with underground garages and places to hide out. Myself and my street duty probationers had the job of searching the estate and underground garages to see if the rumours were true. This was both eerie and scary bearing in mind events just down the road just a short time before. I was relieved to report that we found no evidence of petrol bombs or weapons. However, we were despatched to Tottenham over the next few weeks to patrol the estate with tensions still running high. The place resembled a war zone with rubble, smashed windows and burnt out vehicles scattered throughout the estate.

In 1986 there was another industrial dispute during which I, together with several hundred other officers were caught up in the middle of. This was another failed strike, this time by print workers who tried to blockade distribution of newspapers in Rupert Murdoch's News International Group. A new print works had been set up in Wapping resulting in a lot of workers, who had been using old printing methods, being dismissed. We would form a line across the road leading into the works and struggle to keep the crowds back as the lorries drove in and out. This was referred to as the Wapping dispute and lasted nearly a year although I personally was not there the whole time.

Also, around this time there was a serious overcrowding of prisons and police station cells. Courts were also being used to hold certain categories of prisoners. I had previously had dealings with, and the responsibility for prisoners when a PC at Cheshunt station. This time I was the Sergeant in charge whilst performing this duty at Highbury Corner Magistrates Court. This had a larger cell capacity and therefore substantially more prisoners to secure and take care of. The amount of medication required by the prisoners needed careful attention and at times I felt more like a dispensing chemist or nurse. I am pleased to say that during my time in charge there were no escapes and no deaths.

Highbury Vale police station was a stone's throw, at that time, from the Arsenal football ground so we were always busy on match days. Although I did manage to work inside the ground at some matches, most of the time I was in the charge room at the police station, where prisoners arrested at the ground would be brought for processing and charging. So, my allegiance was changed now as it was the Gunners who were giving me the opportunity to work overtime.

Because us Sergeants were spending so much time in the custody suite and had little opportunity to escape to the canteen for a coffee break, we decided to club together and purchase ourselves a filter coffee machine. This was on the go most of the day and night with coffee on tap as required. I was certainly drinking far too much of it. This was pointed out to me by the Police Doctor who had attended to take a blood sample one-night duty. He was invited to have a cup of coffee but turned it down saying too much coffee was not good for you. I did cut down after that.

I was busy catching up with paperwork one night in the custody suite when the rear door opened and a group of half a dozen or so men entered. Only one was a prisoner who had been arrested for a serious offence and brought to our station due to the tape interview facility we had. The rest were all senior detectives from a central squad. Up until that time all interviews were done by contemporaneously recording questions and answers. Our station was one of the first in the Met. to have had a tape-recording machine installed in the interview room adjacent to the custody area, so the prisoner had been transported to Holloway in order to use the facility. After booking the prisoner in he was escorted into the interview room to be interviewed. I was now alone in the custody suite and proceeded to get on with my outstanding paperwork, amusing myself by whistling a tune or two. After an hour or so the group came out of the interview room and the prisoner released into the escorting officer's custody, to take back to the station he originally came from. The officers thanked me for my assistance and also the whistling that was now background music on the interview tape of their interview for a murder enquiry. Thereafter the interview room was sound proofed, as were all other interview rooms throughout the Met. that were installed with tape recording equipment. I think that this must have been due to the fact that most custody areas were fairly noisy most of the time as opposed to my whistling! It was not unusual to have cell buzzers constantly being pressed, prisoners shouting and screaming from their cells and banging on the doors. This was mostly because they were demanding to see their solicitor or a doctor, wanted a cigarette or they were suffering withdrawal symptoms from drink or drugs.

On one tour of night of duty in the custody suite, I was particularly busy with numerous prisoners to deal with, dozens of items of property and always ended up working over the eight-hour shift in order to clear everything up. Towards the end of one especially busy night I managed to prepare myself for my hand over to the early turn Sergeant. There was just an hour to go when I could hear over the personal radio that there was a car chase locally with four occupants in the car being

131

pursued. Now I would always be rooting for the participants to be captured and be shouting, "Come on lads, catch them." However, I had visions of four prisoners being brought to the station to be processed together with all their property to deal with and a scene of chaos in my currently quiet and calm custody area. I was inwardly shouting, "Don't catch them." Thankfully they left our area and were subsequently apprehended and taken to another station. I did a calculation at the end of the week and counted my signature alone had been written at least 1,600 times and that's without the rest of the entries and reports that had to be handwritten. There were no computers and certainly not the time to type up entries so everything was written in longhand. I decided that I did not wish to do this for the rest of my service.

In January 1987 I was on duty in the front office at Holloway police station when a man entered the station and said, "I want to report two crimes, an arson and criminal damage, I suppose." He then related that he had broken the window of his wife's car, poured petrol inside and set fire to it. He then said that he had gone to the local neighbourhood office and after pushing the front doors in with his car had poured in petrol, threw the can inside and set fire to it. I took him into the charge room, either as a suspect or a nutter. I checked out his story and sure enough he was on the run after these serious arson attacks, another domestic dispute that had got out-of-hand. He was a bit of a pathetic character but I had little or no sympathy for him.

Portrait taken Hendon College

Cadets 1968

Special function

Winning Cross-Country Team

1ˢᵗ weekend at home, showing off

Winning the one mile walk for Herts is cadet M. Trayhorn. His time of 7 mins. 52.8 secs. was a competition record.

Winning 1 Mile Walk

Fancy dress, Whitstable

2nd car, Hillman Minx

Me and Peter

Course 289 Eynsham Hall

Eynsham Hall

Scotland trip with borrowed tent

134

Wedding day

New Sergeant

Trusty steed

My All Aggro

Slapping the cuffs on Charlie Chester

Holloway mug shot

Chapter 14 – Hendon in the Black and Green

It was in February 1986 that I put in an application to become an instructor at Hendon Training School. Later that year I was accepted onto a ten-week instructional techniques course at Hendon training school. During the course I had to prepare and deliver lessons which were assessed by the tutors and more experienced instructors. There were ten of us on the course and those who passed it and considered suitable to be instructors, would be posted in to the training school within three months. This was common practice as it gave time for areas to get permanent replacements. However, most areas did not demand this period of posting-in and the rest of my course mates stayed on after the course and were attached to staff rooms. Not me, I had to return to Holloway and carry on with duties there. This I did for three months and after this time I went to see the Chief Inspector Operations to ask him when I would be released to Hendon. He said that he thought my place was at an operational station and he had kept my application in his drawer. I indicated that I still wished my application to transfer be considered favourably. He said that he would make a deal with me. He stated that he was having problems with a particular relief and it needed a strong Sergeant on the team to sort things out. If I agreed to be attached to that relief for a few weeks, he would see what he could do about my application.

So, it was eventually on 6th April 1987 that I finally arrived at Hendon to start the next part of my police career, as an instructor. There were four staff rooms at the training school and intakes with an average of 180 students. There were 3 instructors designated per two classes with an Inspector in overall charge. Classes were paired and were titled with a letter, A&B, C&D, E&F and G&H. Each intake had a colour, black, blue, yellow and red with each one being at a different stage in a 20-week course. My first period as a probationary instructor was with the black intake and I worked alongside two more experienced instructors. An element of the process of becoming a qualified instructor, in addition to passing the in-house training programme, was to register and provide evidence for the City and Guilds Further and Adult Education Teacher's Certificate (730). I completed this process in April 1988 after giving an assessed lesson to students at an outside college. My lesson was given to English as a second language students, which was interesting and challenging. So, I was now qualified to City and Guilds standard.

After I had been through a couple of 20-week courses I was approached by a Sergeant, who had been an instructor on my initial 10-week instructional techniques course. He asked if I would be interested in joining a new staff room that was being set up. This staff room would be known as the green intake and only selected trainers were being asked to join. I therefore joined a new team which was endearingly referred to as 'The Greenies' or 'The Dream Team.' I went from being a part of a three-person team to being the person in charge of a team. I thoroughly enjoyed this role and delivering lessons to students. I would frequently set up practical situations where I would be the stooge to allow the students to practice skills of controlling incidents in a safe environment. I would dress up as a drunk and even swig some whisky so that I smelt of alcohol and in order to make it as real as possible (that's dedication for you!). I would get someone to video students trying to deal with me being belligerent of just flat out drunk. I would change it each time so the students wouldn't know what they were getting. Sometimes I would be friendly, putting my arms round them and saying things with a slurring sound. "Hello ociffer have a little drinkie with me." Or, "I'm as jober as a sudge and as cadburys as a fudge."

We had a room in the basement set up as a shop for shoplifting practicals and a bed-sit for dealing with sudden deaths. There was a particularly ugly looking fake cadaver that we placed in a bed with a blanket covering it and when the student pulled the blanket back their reactions were priceless. My style of teaching was to keep things simple, explain everything, answer all questions, involve each student and most of all make it fun. I would, on occasions, give a demonstration but the trouble with that is you have to be 100% accurate. My way around this was to tell the students that I was going to demonstrate the correct way to deal with a situation but that I was going to deliberately do something wrong. They were to pay close attention and tell me what the mistake or wrong process was. That way if I missed something or made a mistake, I could cover it by saying, "Well spotted".

On one occasion there was a student who was delegated to deal with a drunk, (me) and he was so weak and useless that it provided me with video proof of the fact that this person would never make a copper as long as he had a hole in his arse. It wasn't just this incident, in case you think I had it in for him, so I brought the matter up with the Chief Inspector who dealt with decisions on whether to keep or dispense with someone. He was all for giving him another chance and I urged him to view the video of him dealing (or not) with the drunk. After the Chief Inspector had seen the video the individual was packed up and, on his way, back to his home town by the end of the afternoon. I firmly believe that I prevented the Metropolitan Police from becoming the laughing stock of the policing world and the individual concerned from ridicule and possible injury. He would have been to the Metropolitan Police the same as the iceberg was to the Titanic!

Another lesson where I would dress up was dealing with someone with a mental illness. I would dress up in odd clothing, have lots of watches up my arms and lots of pens in pockets of a shirt and jacket. I would lock myself in the gent's toilet and start making strange noises and saying weird things. The student would be told that a call had been received to someone acting strangely in the toilets and they would be sent in to deal. I had based the character on people that I had dealt with in the past and although it created some humour it allowed students to practice something that they may well have to deal with themselves in the future. I got a bit of a reputation for playing this role and had many requests from other instructors to perform it for their students.

The recruits were required to attend shield training exercises at a specially constructed site in Hounslow, West London, during their course. This had a mock-up of houses and streets a bit like a film set, most of them just being the facade of a building. Although, as an instructor I was not required to participate, I always did join in. In riot helmets with visors and flame-retardant overalls we would be deployed, with a long shield, around the streets until we came across a rioting mob. This consisted of another bunch of recruits and shield training instructors shouting and making threatening moves towards the thin blue line of shield carrying police. The threat level was raised from shouting to throwing big chunks of wood at us. Although not rocks or bricks they didn't half hurt if they made contact with you! This would last for some time with us clearing streets of demonstrators and continually getting wooden blocks thrown at us. It is surprising in these circumstances how quickly you learn how to use the shields to protect yourself and also work as a team. We got to have our own back on the other group by throwing blocks at them when they were practising with the shields. Another exercise was to use the shields in small groups to enter a premises and corner a violent suspect in a room in order to arrest him. After a demonstration of how to deal with a petrol bomb coming at you, we experienced this for ourselves. You can certainly feel the heat, even whilst screened behind the shield and if you haven't got it completely on the ground, the flames would get underneath and your boots start to smoulder.

The exercise would always finish at the end of the day with a shield run. This would mean you running in full riot gear, carrying your shield around the site on a designated route. In order to pass this test, you had to achieve the distance within two minutes. Not all recruits managed this but I am proud to say that not only did I beat the two minutes but most of the recruits as well. I can assure you that running in that gear was not easy and the shield cumbersome and heavy! I was thankful that I was now prepared for any future major public disorder events but couldn't help thinking that it would have been useful when I needed it most as a PC during the incidents I had encountered during the eighties.

As an exercise in meeting the public and also to assist with crowd control in a non-conflict situation our intake was requested to assist at the London Marathon. After briefing students in what to do if approached by a member of the public and receiving any found property, we travelled in coaches from Hendon to central London. I was in charge of a class of recruits that was designated to look after a crossing point in Northumberland Avenue. This involved keeping the large crowds behind a roped off section until there were sufficient numbers that wished to cross to the other side of the road. The runners would then be diverted to the opposite carriageway so that we could facilitate people crossing half way. The runners then would be diverted back to the original carriageway and people could complete their crossing. This required precision timing and strict control of the crowds. I had possession of a loud hailer, which I used to issue instructions to the crowds. I also encouraged the crowds to cheer on the runners plus cracking a few funnies to keep people in good humour. When we got back on the coach at the end of the day, one of the recruits came up to me and said that a member of a public had asked him if I was really a police officer. Well I couldn't pass up an opportunity to entertain a crowd, could I?

I like to think that the lessons I gave were lively and informative even though some of the subject areas were quite dry. However, I am well aware that students find it hard to focus at times, especially in those sessions after lunch. I was in mid flow one afternoon when I noticed one of the student's heads starting to flop forward and his eyes closing. I initially ignored it and pretended I hadn't seen it. The other members of the class had seen him and were sniggering and looking towards me to see when I would say something. It would be true to say that he was not the most popular member of the class and I was sure that they would dearly love to have seen him being chastised. I finished the lesson and dismissed the class but asked the sleeping student to stay behind. I asked him if there was a reason why he was having difficulty maintaining attention. This was to establish if there were any welfare issues that applied before admonishing him for falling asleep during one of my lessons. He apologised profusely and off he went. The next day he turned up at the staff room door with a letter addressed to me. It read: -

P.S. Trayhorn

I apologise for the embarrassment caused to you by falling asleep during your lesson yesterday. I do not find any of your lessons boring in any way, and believe that my sleeping in class was called by too many late nights. I intend to rectify this problem as of now. I hope that this will be the last occasion that I waste your time through my own stupidity.

Sincerely Yours (signature)

I have always kept this letter as a reminder to me that my lessons might not always be as entertaining or interesting as I would like plus the fact that some students are absolute plonkers!

One of the members of the team I led was George, a Constable of many years' experience and a lot older than me. If I had been in class teaching and he was in the staff room preparing lessons he would see me come into the room and would pick up a small gold coloured bell he kept on his desk. He would ring it and say, "Tea Sergeant, one sugar." So it was that I became the tea boy. When George was eventually posted elsewhere, he had a leaving do in the staff bar and he came up to me with a gift-wrapped parcel and presented it to me. I was really touched and when I opened it, I found it contained the gold bell. I still have it to this day (You're not surprised, are you?) George was a true gentleman, good fun to be with, a good instructor and great friend. He went on to become a Sergeant but sadly a few years later he passed away.

At Christmas it was traditional to put on a concert to celebrate the festive season plus bring some light relief to the intensity of the course for the students. Most classes put on either a musical rendering or a sketch. It was surprising how much talent there was amongst the students, and staff for that matter. The Greenies instructors decided to put on a short melodrama called the 'D' Drama. It was so titled because all the characters and the whole script started with the letter 'D'. My character was a policeman called, "Dixon Dock -Don't!" I still remember my last line, which was, "Dixon Discovered Dirty Dick Driving Deluxe Dormobile Down Deptford Docks, Dixon Decided Dirty Dick Deserved Ducking, Dixon Diverted Deluxe Dormobile Down Dockside. Dirty Dick Dived Deep, Didn't Drown, Dixon Detained Desperado." This was an absolute hoot and, on my recommendation, it has since been used by two of my drama groups. The following year when I was in the Blues we put on a rather silly rendering of, 'There's a one-eyed yellow idol to the north of Khatmandu'. I have not recommended that to anyone else because it was pretty rubbish really.

A new female Inspector (Ma'am Payne) took charge of the Greenies after our original male Inspector had been promoted and was moving on. The Inspector in charge of staff rooms always had a Sergeant as a deputy to represent them when they were absent and as our Sergeant deputy had also moved to another post, there was a vacancy. I was recommended by the outgoing Inspector so now was not only team leader but also Deputy Intake Manager, or D.I.M. I was never sure after that, when someone called me DIM whether it was because of my position or that I was not too bright?!

One task I took on was organising the end of course dining out night. This involved lots of organising. One task was to arrange for dress hire companies for men and women, to come to Hendon and measure up those who wished to hire appropriate attire for the event. I always managed to get mine at no cost, not surprisingly! Another was to find a venue that could cater for up to 500 people at a sit-down formal black-tie dinner. The nearest place that tended to be used was a large hotel near to London Airport. This meant that coaches needed to be arranged to transport everyone to the venue and then back again at the end of the evening. I arranged to meet the hotel manager some weeks before the due date and run through what we required. The theme was green to match the intake colour so green coloured napkins for the tables were asked for as well as a room to hold a sherry reception for VIP guests. I requested that there be plenty of vegetables available especially as they were charging a large amount for the meal. All arrangements were agreed and I had meetings with the class Captains of the intake to get menu choices and agree arrangements.

On the night things were not as had been requested, they had not set up the sherry reception correctly and the meal was less than average with small portions and not enough vegetables to go round. The head waiter came up to me during the meal and made the mistake of asking me if everything was alright. I then let loose with all the things that were wrong and that they had not done as requested and agreed. "I'm very sorry Mr. Malcolm, I will let the Hotel manager know." A few minutes later the Hotel manager appeared and said, "I am sorry that you are not happy let me get you two bottles of champagne for your table." Not the right thing to say! I said, "If you think you can bribe me with two bottles of champagne you have got another thing coming." I sent him off after telling him what I thought of his Hotel. I submitted a full report listing everything that had gone wrong with the booking and at the event. I subsequently had a meeting with the Commandant at Hendon and as a result the Hotel were informed that we would not be using them again. A massive loss of potential income of at least £20,000 every five weeks. Don't mess with me matey!

I had the idea of introducing the recruits to all the different societies there were in the Met, prior to going out to their stations. There were numerous Metropolitan Police Athletic Association (MPAA) groups only too interested to get new members to join them. I contacted as many of them as I could and arranged an evening for them all to come to a room at Hendon where the recruits could come along and find out more. There was lots of interest and this event took place on a few occasions with groups from rugby, football, diving, badminton, chess and archery, to name but a few.

The passing out parades the day after dining out night were held at the parade square at what used to be the cadet end of the Hendon site. The students had received a number of sessions with the drill Sergeant to ensure that they could march to a reasonable standard. There would be a band and sometimes police horses would appear. All the parents, friends and VIP guests would sit around the outside of the square and the students would march out behind the band, led by the intake Inspector and the course instructors. The reviewing officer would be of a senior rank, usually the Commissioner, a visiting Chief Constable, a politician or occasionally a Royal. Ma'am Payne, our Inspector, hated having to lead out the parade and so handed that honour over to her deputy, me! I always enjoyed this task and was filled with pride for the intake and myself when taking the salute. My hours of marching backwards and forwards on the parade square at Hertfordshire Constabulary when a cadet had paid off!

Another thing I must say about the Greenies before I move on and to reinforce what a strong team we were is to mention the annual yachting trips. These started as one of our team, Barry, was a keen sailor and suggested that we have a team outing down to the river Hamble in Hampshire. We hired a mini-bus to take us to Hampshire where hired yacht for the day. After boarding with all our gear, we would set sail and venture out into the Solent. After a stop for lunch in Cowes or somewhere along the coast, we would sail back arriving late in the afternoon. We would shower and change into our best clobber before going to the Royal Yacht Club for a celebratory glass of bubbly and a sit-down meal. This was such a special day that we made it an annual event the last one being held in 1995.

Part of my job as D.I.M. was to cover any lesson where an instructor was off sick or on leave. During a twenty-week course I built up a very good rapport with the classes of students and as deputy also with most classes. The students always liked to show their appreciation and I received many gifts over those years. These included: – A pair of cut crystal glasses in a presentation box, a cut crystal decanter, an inscribed tankard, a watch, an inscribed carriage clock, an inscribed gold pen and numerous bottles of whisky.

The inscriptions on the tankard read: -

Presented to Sgt. M. TRAYHORN By 7/87 G Class Jan 1988
With Gratitude for your Endeavour

Chapter 15 – The Blues and T. S. U.

I can't remember how it came about now, but on 31st July 1989, I moved over to the Blue intake staff room and became the Deputy Intake Manager (D.I.M.) there for a while. Each staff room also had a representative who was responsible for the progress and development of new members of staff. This meant liaising with the staff development unit. Because everything seemed to have an acronym it made me the Staff Development Liaison Officer or S.D.L.O. As I had two roles the acronyms were mashed together and thereafter, I was known as a D.I.L.D.O or Deputy Intake Liaison Development Officer. I was beginning to think that I would never be taken seriously!

We had a visit one day from an Inspector, who was covering for one of the senior officers along the first corridor. He was asking me for a favour, I can't remember what it was, I said I was only too happy to help but never ever get a well done. He immediately got a piece of paper from his file, wrote WELL DONE on it in capital letters, signed it and gave it to me. I still have this note together with the one that arrived from him the next day. It said: -

Dear Mal, further to my 'well done' note, I have reconsidered the repercussions of my rash act. However, I would agree that as a D.I.L.D.O. you are eminently qualified I cannot in all honesty let you aspire to a 'well done', I therefore retract any such leakage. Love (Signature)

It was also about this time that I was involved with others in setting up Skills Evaluation Exercises (SEE's). It was felt that the recruits were being tested purely on their knowledge with the tests but not tested on their ability to deal with situations practically. We devised practical exercises and set up practical rooms on a floor in one of the tower blocks. The recruits were given a briefing sheet which they read before entering each room and had a specified amount of time to display their skills which were observed and scored. This concept was further developed and a purpose-built village erected on site for skills testing. My Brother-in-Law, Tim, was later to become the Sergeant in charge of this village.

An opportunity to earn overtime at Hendon was to be involved in the training of Special Constables at weekends. These courses lasted a number of weeks, after which there was a social function and a passing out parade. Although I had never really agreed with the concept of Specials in modern policing myself I have to admit that the groups I had were dedicated and great bunch of individuals who genuinely wanted to support the regular officers. They were equally appreciative of our efforts and I received tankards and bottles as a token of their thanks.

The inscriptions on the tankards read: -

To SGT. TRAYHORN Many Thanks from MSC Class 3/89
Presented to Malcolm Trayhorn from MSC 5/90 B The A Team

It was not a lot longer after that I was approached by a member of the Training Support Unit (TSU or as it was more commonly called, the 'Thick Shit Unit') and asked if I would be interested in working with them. This unit had been set up to support and assist those students who were struggling with the lessons and exams. The unit consisted of an Inspector in overall charge with a Sergeant and four P.C.s. The current Sergeant was being posted out, having passed his Inspector's exam and being promoted, so they were short a Sergeant. The P.C.s were, Dave, Frank, Stuart and another Dave (nickname Scooby), who said that they had chosen me to approach as they thought they could work with me. My belief is that they chose me because they thought I could be manipulated to their way of working (they were right).

However, I did move over to this position on 21st August 1989, which proved to be one of the best moves I ever made. Dave and Frank taught me everything about helping students including study skills and exam technique. One of the suggestions that we made to students was to learn certain definitions by heart. This being useful to bring to mind the relevant points to prove for offences. There was a bank of computers in the TSU room that students could use during breaks and in the evenings. These had learning programmes on them which reinforced information and explained offences in simplified terms and with examples.

One of the senior officers, a Superintendent, visited one day to see what the unit did. He said that he was not an advocate of learning things by heart, preferring that people learnt as they went along. Dave sat him down on one of the computers and set him up with a programme relating to burglary. A question appeared which required a response relating to the points to prove for the offence. The Superintendent stopped and looked up for a moment towards the ceiling. Dave asked him what he was doing. He said, "I am just recalling the definition of burglary, Oh! Now I see what you mean." He left a bit embarrassed but we hoped a little wiser.

We would also give more in-depth or simplified explanations to lessons. It did mean that one of us would work late in the evenings to cover this facility. I would often be asked, "Are you working late tonight Sergeant?" I recall one student, who said that he was confused after a lesson on powers of arrest that he had attended earlier that day. After I went through powers of arrest with him and explained each element, he said, "Why didn't anyone tell me about this?" Often there would be several students sitting round at the end of the room listening to explanations about powers of arrest, theft, burglary or many other subjects. I would book a room in one of the tower blocks and stay overnight.

It was rumoured that the corridors, basement area and rooms in the tower blocks were rife with intimate liaisons between male and female students, but I have to say I never witnessed this. I was the youngest member of the team and was referred to as, 'The Boy', when there were no students about. We were such a close-knit team that we used to have games nights round each other's houses, together with wives. One of the jobs that befell the TSU staff was to assist at the passing out parades. We used to oversee the arrangements on the day, briefing class captains from the following intake as to their duties. This involved having someone at key points to guide people or prevent them from entering areas reserved for V.I.P.'s as well as being on-hand at the edge of the parade square to deal with any student who fainted whilst standing to attention in the heat for too long. I would rush on with a stretcher, together with another, to take the prone person off to receive first aid and recover sufficiently to re-join the parade. There is no doubt that the success of these parades was in no small part due to the meticulous organising by our team, especially Dave and Frank. The Commandant would regularly invite the three of us round to his office for a drink at the end of the day to thank us.

One day, whilst sitting in our little tea corner in the office, Ray, the Sergeant who was in charge of the administration team, along what we knew as the first floor, came in to ask for a favour. The first-floor corridor was where the Chief Superintendent (Commandant), the Superintendent and the Chief Inspector were situated. He said that he was due to go on holiday and needed someone he could trust to look after things along the first-floor corridor whilst he was away. I reluctantly agreed and he showed me what he wanted doing. This mostly consisted of filtering the incoming mail to the respective senior officer's in-box. Once it had been dealt with Ray would take any required actions, get the admin staff to type up any replies and get them sent off. This was fine until I was going through the mail in the in-tray one day and when I reached near to the bottom, I found a letter which was dated some time previous and the content looked to be contentious. I had no idea what to do with it so I hid it in a drawer until Ray came back from holiday. When he did and I pointed it out to him, he said, "Oh that, I should have warned you about that don't worry you have to know when to leave some things alone until they go away." The next time he went on holiday and I was going through the mail in the in-tray I reached a piece of paper that said, 'Malcolm it is dangerous to go any further than this!' (I never kept that one!)

Another time whilst in the tea corner an instructor from one of the staff rooms came in to ask me a favour, I think I must have had, 'Mug' written across my forehead! He asked that as I had been invited as a guest to their dining out night, would I be prepared to deliver the response speech on behalf of the guests? As we helped out so many students it was not unusual for us to be invited but the speech in question would normally be given by a parent, usually a prominent member of the armed forces or profession. Apparently, the person who was to have given the speech had contacted them to say that they were now unable to attend and so needed someone at short notice. I disappeared down to the library to put something together and with jittery nerves I stood up to give my response after the student's excellent speech welcoming the guests and thanking the instructional staff for their efforts over the proceeding twenty weeks. I gave a response on behalf of all the guests, thanking the recruits for inviting us to their special evening and wishing them luck in their future career. I composed this speech entirely in rhyme. It seemed to get a good response with lots of laughter and a good round of applause at the end. I had lots of people come up to me afterwards to congratulate me. It couldn't have been too bad as I was asked to do it again three more times during my time at the training school. (Copies kept!)

Around this time the Metropolitan Police were producing a new recruitment magazine and wanted some pictures taken at Hendon to put in it. I was chosen to pose for a picture with a young female recruit to show a caring manner. How many of these brochures that were distributed, I've no idea but I certainly have a copy!

It was also whilst attached to the TSU that I got demoted to a PC and had occasion to, 'arrest' Gary Wilmot. A film team had arrived at Hendon where they wanted to film excerpts for a children's television programme. One of the scenes required a police officer arresting Gary and leading him away. The only issue was that the arresting officer needed to be a PC, so I had to don a borrowed tunic and revert to being a PC. The filming took place out on the training roads and after a few takes they were happy with the results. We were told that we would be informed when the programme was to be broadcast but we never were. If the programme was ever aired, I never heard. It probably ended up on the cutting room floor. That was the end of my TV career but meeting Gary Wilmot was a good experience and he was a gentleman and a very nice person.

I must have become the person to go to for favours as I was approached one day by someone from the Yellow intake asking if I would drive the mini-bus with a group of recruits and trainers to Wales. They had organised a charity trip to walk to the top of Snowdon and needed a driver to take them to Wales. I did drive them there, camped out overnight and also walked with them up Snowdon (So that was the second time I had been to the top of this mountain).

Whilst I was attached to the T.S.U. in 1990 it was discussed that there should be an Instructors charity walk to raise money for the North London Hospice Appeal. Plans were made and on the 1st July 1990 eight of us set off in a borrowed mini-bus to the Lake District. We managed to get one that was used in riot situations with a grill that comes down to protect the windscreen and driver. The challenge was to climb twelve peaks in six days. The mini-bus was adorned with transfers which said, 'Plod for Charity', 'Metropolitan Police Instructors Charity Walk', Twelve Peaks in six days' and 'In Aid of North London Hospice Appeal'. We loaded the bus with provisions that were donated by companies that supplied the school's canteen. Throughout the journey and walk we collected donations from everyone we bumped into. People were very generous, including pub landlords, allowing us to collect from their customers plus motorway service stations and people out walking in Cumbria. The twelve peaks were, Green Gable, Great Gable, Knowe Craggs, Hallsfell Top, SaddleBack, Foule Cragg, Dolly Wagon Pike, Nethermost Pike, Helvellyn, Little Man, Skiddaw and Scafell Pike. (So that was the second time I had been up the highest mountain in England only this time in better weather).

We all became fully paid up members of the Youth Hostelling Association and so stayed overnight in Youth Hostels along the way. We topped up any fluid lost during the day in local hostelries. Someone was designated as driver each day and it was his job to meet us at an appropriate spot en-route, or at the end, to hand out refreshments and convey us back to a Hostel. I was still, 'The Boy' and on one climb was ribbed due to the amount of stuff I carried in my ruck sack. Snacks, oranges, emergency rations, binoculars, camera and extra waterproof clothing mainly. I had to admit that I found it did weigh me down as we climbed and seemed to feel heavier the more we went on. It wasn't until we reached the peak and I opened up my ruck sack that I found a number of rocks inside. My fellow hikers had been putting rocks in the ruck sack every time we had stopped for a break without me noticing. I called them rude names and they were in fits of laughter. Carrying extra rations and clothing proved to be the right thing however. Whilst climbing up another peak we encountered sudden bad weather. The clouds came down and it turned very cold. You couldn't see very far in front of you and we relied on our map and compass skills to find our way. We came across a group of school children on the path who were being led by their teacher. They were trying to shelter from the weather behind some rocks. They were ill equipped, did not have suitable clothing, footwear or any rations. The teacher was actually the worst off and was suffering from hypothermia. We set to and made hot soup with our flasks of hot water and powdered soup packets. We also had emergency chocolate bars and handed over our extra clothing. We had to put the teacher in a survival bag to warm him up and stop him deteriorating any further. After a while the weather improved slightly and we escorted the group back down the mountain to safety.

We found a pub at the foot of the mountain and the landlord opened up for us, allowing us to dry off and warm up by a roaring open fire. Our support driver arrived and drove the school party back to their Hostel while we stopped at the pub. We reflected on our hero status as well as downing copious amounts of reviving fluids! This was a very enjoyable six days and we had a great time as well as raising money for the charity. It was still bloody hard work though!

In 1991 it was decided that we should have another Metropolitan Police Instructors plod for charity. This time we were to walk the West Highland Way in aid of Cot Death Research. With a couple of changes there were the same suspects on this outing with a suitably festooned mini-bus. Again, we stayed in Youth Hostels along the way and took it in turns to drive the support vehicle. This time we had radios lent to us by a company that supplies operational police radios, which allowed us to communicate with the support vehicle. At the end of this walk we decided to climb Ben Nevis (So now I had climbed all three highest mountains in England, Wales and Scotland).

As our walks were becoming an annual event, the next venture in June of 1992 was to walk the, 'Coast to Coast', route from Bees Head in the West to Robin Hood's Bay in the East, a distance of ninety-six miles. There had been a change of Commander at the training school so we weren't sure that we would get permission. Another problem was that the school's mini-bus was not available for the period we had planned. Not only did the Commander agree to the venture but assisted us with getting transport and even had his driver take him to our start location, where he stayed in a hotel overnight, met us for a drink the night before and walked with us for the whole of the first day. I can't remember what charity we walked for that year as I can't find any reference of it. We did very well that year with supplying numerous walkers on the route with food and drink as they passed by our support vehicle whilst it was awaiting our arrival. We had plenty of supplies so this arrangement worked well and I think the Commander was very impressed with our organisation and public relations building that took place. The Commander in question was John Grieve a thoroughly nice man and great leader. He went on to do many great things during his police career and after retiring became a university lecturer and a member of the Independent Monitoring Commission that monitors the Northern Ireland peace process. He was awarded the CBE and QPM.

We did, in fact, pick up an extra member of the team on our route as we came across a 62-year-old man who had been walking with two other people who had given up. He had been left alone so we adopted him, or he adopted us, I'm not sure which. He sent a very complimentary letter of thanks after the trip of which I still have a copy (of course!) Seven days into the walk, tragedy struck when I had a call from home telling me that Barbara had been taken ill and had been admitted to hospital. The next day I was on a train from Darlington back home. Thankfully Barbara was fine and released from hospital after what would appear to have been a false alarm. I had missed the last four days of the walk so can't say that I completed the Coast to Coast walk. I was always still referred to as, 'The Boy' on these trips, although I'm not sure if I was actually the youngest?

First instituted in 1951, police officers in the United Kingdom receive a 'Long Service and Good Conduct Medal', after twenty years of service. I became eligible in terms of the twenty years and I believe also for good conduct. In my experience and from a lot of things I had witnessed over the years there were a lot of officers who may have survived the twenty years but were not and had not been of good conduct. I knew of several officers who refused their medals because they knew of recipients who they believed not to be worthy thereby, in their view, devaluing its worth. Others refused to attend any official presentation ceremony and asked for it to be sent to them by despatch. However, on 12th March 1993 I attended the ceremony held at the Simpson Hall, Hendon where numerous officers were presented with their medals by the new Commissioner, Sir Paul Condon. It was actually a really good day and my Father, Mother and Barbara attended to witness the moment. Another Memento for my collection!

Chapter 16 – Marathon Malc

Whilst at Hendon I maintained a good standard of physical fitness and would go on lunchtime runs or swimming in the Hendon pool. The facilities were excellent at the site and I made use of them whilst I was there. I decided in 1991 that I would apply for entrance to the London marathon and started to train up for longer distances. On a Sunday Barbara would take me out in the car and when the milometer got to ten miles, she would drop me off to run home. Eventually she would drop me off twenty miles from home. In March I did a half marathon at St Edmunds College in a time of 1hr. 40mins, also the Hitchin Hard Half marathon in a time of 1hr. 40mins 26seconds.

Because it was my first marathon and the advice was that you should walk the route before attempting the distance, Barbara and I went to London the week before the race and walked the route. It took us 9hrs 18mins. When Barbara got off the train she could hardly walk. The following Sunday I turned up at the designated rendezvous point and waited for the start. Drink plenty of water was the advice I was given, so I knocked back lots of it to keep me going through the 26.2miles to come. That year the run was sponsored by ADT but I was running for the Cot Death Charity. I started off feeling fine, even though it took several minutes to reach the start line after the starting gun had been sounded, due to the thousands of runners. I found it difficult to keep to any steady pace due to the number of runners and either having to dodge past slower runners or get out of the way of faster ones. After only a mile or so I felt the need to go for a pee as my bladder was fit to burst. I desperately looked for somewhere that I could sneak behind to relieve myself but couldn't readily see anywhere. I shouldn't have worried because as I turned the next corner there was a block of flats with a large green area in front of it. There were dozens of runners who were obviously feeling the same as me because there were fountains of pee emanating up against walls, trees and hedges. It wasn't restricted to men either, there were women squatting quite openly and unashamedly relieving themselves.

Much later in the run I had a churning rumble in my stomach and desperately need to visit a lavatory. I eventually came across a row of mobile toilets and after queueing up for a short time got myself more comfortable. Twenty miles was reasonable going and a distance that I had trained for, but the last six miles I had not. When I got to the embankment and only a couple of miles or so to go, I hit, 'The Wall' and just had to stop and walk. My legs had given up on me and a kindly St. Johns Ambulance man, seeing my plight massaged my legs with Vaseline. As I slowly walked on there was a shout from someone at the side of the road saying, "Come on if you lot keep going you are still on for the four hours". This spurred me on and I managed to get back into a slow run. I turned the corner into Northumberland Avenue and suddenly heard a familiar voice shout, "Come on Malcolm Trayhorn!" It was a lady Chief Inspector from the training school and so I put on a bit of a spurt. She told me afterwards that I was going really well when I passed her. Little did she know how I was a few minutes earlier!

My overall finish position was 12,900 and 2,388 within my age group and sex. The time recorded as I crossed the line was 4hrs 3mins. 32 secs. But taking off the time it took me to get to the start my stop watch showed a time of 3hrs 55mins. So just under the 4hrs. On that day it was me who had trouble walking from the train.

Chapter 17 – Area Training

After five years spent at Hendon (2 years in staff rooms and 3 years in T.S.U.) it was time for me to return to Division. At my leaving do at the instructor's bar at Hendon I was presented with another tankard with the inscription: -

Malcolm Trayhorn Presented for dedicated Service at Police Training School Hendon
26-4-87 - 4-5-92 From all your colleagues and friends

I was to return to Ponders End police station and straight back into a training role. A Sergeant in the Area Training Unit there was due to give birth and go on maternity leave and so on 5th May of 1992, I joined a small training unit consisting of 5 training staff. I was involved in the continuation training of probationers and many other courses such as, Civilian Station Reception Officers, Special Constables, Civil Staff in process admin. and crime support units, pre-trial issues, custody officers' courses, P.C. to P.S. promotion classes to name but a few. Ponders End is 8 miles from where we lived in Broxbourne and I would cycle there most days but, on a Friday, I would run in and then home again at the end of the day. I had a change of clothes at the station or in my ruck sack and would shower at the station. The run one way would take me just under an hour.

I decided at this time to further my teaching qualification and applied to take the Certificate in Education as a day release course at Greenwich University. I was allowed to attend each Monday for the next year and travelled to the Wapping campus for lectures. I found this course so different than the City and Guilds but was glad that I had done that first because that accounted for a year of the two-year Certificate in Education course. I did lots of reading, research and study for this course and submitted a number of written papers. The course was all about the models of teaching plus the wider concepts of teaching and although interesting to a point, didn't really cover the practicality and challenges faced on a daily basis in a classroom environment. I was awarded the Certificate in Education (Post Compulsory Education and Training- P.C.E.T.) on 28th September 1993. Barbara attended the presentation ceremony at the Central Hall Westminster on 15th November. I received the scroll wearing the customary gown and mortar board and now have letters after my name, Malcolm Kenneth Trayhorn CertEd.

In October 1993 the Area Training Unit was moved to Chigwell police station and so my journey was now 13 miles each way from home. I did cycle once a week but as there were a few steep hills it was not a journey to cycle every day and certainly not suitable for a run. The courses continued here as before and then one day I received a request to assist an officer who had spent some years away from front line policing as a courts officer. It turned out that he was not the only one in this position, as the policy at that time was to move personnel about after 5 years in a post. There were people working in courts, mounted branch, special branch, traffic and other areas who had been in those posts for many years. What they knew about their specialist areas was outstanding, what they knew about front line every day policing left a lot to be desired. I proposed a two-day workshop for those officers to assist them in identifying their weak areas, discuss with them a strategy for learning plus provide them with the distance learning material, as supplied to recruits at the training school.

I thought the concept was great, getting those attending to take responsibility for their own learning, very contemporary! Or so I thought. On the first morning I explained the concept to the gathered audience of mid to long serving officers. I was to get a unanimous tirade of displeasure that the day was not to teach them but direct them as to identify areas they needed to get up-to-date with. "I thought we were coming here to learn something." was one remark and others that were less complimentary. I said, "O.K. You tell me what you want me to teach you in the next two days, I'll list them on a flip chart and while you go and have a tea break, I will see what I can put together." I had a long list of subjects such as, powers of arrest, cautioning, the Police and Criminal Evidence Act codes of practice, the Vehicle Defect

Rectification Scheme, issuing fixed penalty notices to name but a few. After Tea break, I said, "Right pin back your lug 'oles and cop a load of this!" I spent the rest of the two days covering as much information as I could and at the end, I got so much appreciation and thanks that I reported to the Inspector that we needed to run a week course for such officers. So, the Legislation Procedure and Update Course, or as it was more commonly called, the 'Back to the Future' course, was formulated.

I had a year off from marathon running and after finishing it in 1992, I said that I would never do it again. However, I was still running regularly and decided in 1993 to apply again for the 1994 London Marathon. I got a place and so was seriously preparing myself for it now being a bit wiser. I ran in three half marathons on the lead up to the London event. The first was Roding Valley on 27th February, where my time was 1 Hour 40 Minutes and 26 Seconds. The second was the Hitchin Hard Half on 6th March where my time was 1 Hour 39 Minutes and 13 Seconds. The third was at St. Edmunds College, where my time was 1 Hour 38 Minutes and 5 Seconds. I was now ready for the big event and turned up on Sunday 17th April 1994 for my second Marathon. This one was sponsored by Nutrasweet and I was running for the Motor Neurone Disease Charity. Things went pretty much according to plan this time and I finished in 3 Hours 47 Minutes and 1 Second. My overall position was 10906 and 1904 for my age & sex. I managed to collect £1,465 in sponsorship money for Motor Neurone Disease Association.

After a year and a half at the Area Training Unit I made an application to attend a six-week residential training course in Bedfordshire. This was a Home Office approved course to prepare experienced police trainers to deliver community & race relations plus equal opportunities training. This was run by Equalities Associates from the Laws Hotel in a small village called Turvey in Bedfordshire. The owner was a very charismatic character called Jerome Mack who was an American. He had a number of staff to help him run the Hotel and the course which consisted of police personnel from around the country.

On my course there were sixteen delegates from various forces: – Norfolk, Lincolnshire, Cambridgeshire, Greater Manchester, Tayside, North Wales, The Met., West Yorkshire, West Mercia, Merseyside, Lothian & Borders, Dyfed Powys and Hertfordshire. This was a very intense six weeks with a full time-table and only broken at weekends when we could escape home for a couple of days. During the course there were many challenges and soul searching by all of us as we were guided through the process of discussing and questioning our perceptions and stereotypes. There were some that really got emotional at times and even had to leave the room in tears. We had visits from members of the African Caribbean, Asian and Traveller communities amongst others. Each told of their experiences of living in England and encounters they had experienced with the police. A part of the course was to spend a weekend with a minority ethnic family in the community to experience their life styles and ask questions. Some were billeted with Asian families but I was to stay with an African Caribbean family.

The family I stayed with lived in Peterborough in a mid-terrace house. The lady, Joyce, was on her own at the time with three of her children. They originated from Jamaica and her Husband was out there at the time I stayed so I never met him. She was a large and kindly lady who was very laid back. Not only did she have her own children, some grown up, but she also fostered children. I was given a bedroom to stay in and her son, Robert, who was in his teens took me round the area showing me round and telling me his experiences with the police. Joyce was a fabulous cook and I swear I put on lots of weight that weekend with fried chicken and rice plus Akee and salt fish.

On the Saturday night we were picked up in an old ambulance to spend an evening at an African Caribbean club in the centre of Peterborough. There was also another of our group, who was staying with another local family. On the way there we were drinking Caribbean milk punch laced with plenty of rum. At the club we were the only white faces present but were made to feel very welcome and invited to join in all activities. We left there very merry having been dancing and singing and drinking all night.

When our group all met up at the end of the weekend, we were told by those staying with Asian families that they spent most of the weekend watching their hosts praying. As they were Muslims, they had not had a sniff of any alcohol and were so thankful that the weekend had come to an end. I remained in contact with Joyce and her family for many years, although never actually visited them again. Joyce did ring me a couple of years later in tears saying that her son had been killed. "Malcolm, they killed my boy, they killed my Robert." I discovered that this was drug related but did not find out what his involvement had been. Joyce was distraught and all I could do was listen and try to sympathise with her. The course finished on 27th May 1994.

On my return I went back to delivering the same training as previously with no sign of being used for the type of courses for which I had been prepared for six long weeks. I came out of class one day and walking into the staff room came face to face with the Commander, who was making a visit to the unit. When he saw me, he looked at my name badge and said, "Ah Trayhorn you've been to Turvey haven't you?" I said, "Yes Sir." He said, "So you are a very expensive commodity, aren't you?" I said, "Yes sir I suppose I am." He said, "So in round figures how cost effective are you?" I said, "In round figures, zero sir." He looked at me quizzically and said, "What do you mean?" I said, "Well, I have been back from Turvey for over a year and haven't been used once for any equal opportunities or race relations training." "Point taken." He said and then left. I heard nothing more about the encounter or indeed was still not given any such training to deliver whilst in the Metropolitan Police.

The Chief Inspector in charge of the Area Training Unit was a strong advocate of the tenure policy and as I now had four years within the unit, he was already telling me that I needed to consider my next posting. I spoke to someone in the postings office to request that I could be posted somewhere nearer to home as it was my last posting before retirement. The reply that came back was that I would be posted to central London or Stoke Newington. This was not in my plans and although I still had a few months before being moved, I started to consider other options. Somebody pointed out that they were advertising in police orders for applicants to join the Training Design and Research Unit (TDRU) at Hendon as a, 'white note' writer. This was the distance learning material that was given to recruits and which I had been supplying to the 'Back to the Future' delegates, so I thought that it would be a good option and after all I knew my way to Hendon.

So it was that I applied for the post and after an interview and assessment, was accepted. When the Chief Inspector found out he was furious with me saying that he was relying on me to help deliver a new course for Sergeants. I pointed out that he was the person who was so keen on people moving on after five years in accordance with the tenure policy. He said, "Why does everyone take me so literally." I started to say something but stopped. He said, "No, go on say what you were going to say." I said, "Well you know what it's like when someone gets religion and they have to try and convert everyone else? That's what you are like with tenure. I wish to have control over where I spend my last posting and have no intention of going to Central London or Stoke Newington."

At my leaving do from this posting I was presented with a tankard that was engraved with: -

'Tappy Trayhorn' Late of this Unit
Date In : 5-5-92 Date Out : 1-9-96

The reference to 'Tappy' was due to me having taken up tap dancing around this time (more about this later).

The Chief Inspector sent me a very nice letter, thanking me for my dedication to the Area Training Unit and especially for designing and running the 'Back to the Future' courses. He also wished me good luck in my new posting, so not such a bad guy after all!

Chapter 18 – Farrow House – White Notes and Exams

So it was that on 2nd September 1996 I returned to Hendon to train as a white note (distance learning material) writer in the Training Design and Research Unit (TDRU). This experience, I have to say was a frustrating one, mostly because I was put under the guidance of a long winded and exasperating tutor. Doug had been a trainer at the recruit training side of Hendon, so had a good knowledge of how students learned through the material supplied. I was given a title for a set of notes on which to practice, which was, 'Protecting yourself from infectious diseases.'

This process took many months, not just because of the amount of research required or the gathering of information or the consultation with medical people or the actual writing, but because of trying to pin Doug down to finalise anything. Doug would invariably arrive late with some feeble excuse and the first task was to have breakfast in the canteen. He had such a reputation for being late that the lads in the office produced a list of 32 excuses for him to use. Here are a few: -

- *Abduction by extra-terrestrials ("I lost half an hour. Look, even my watch is 30 minutes slow!")*

- *Annual Wildebeest migration crossing the Serengeti by means of a short diversion through Brentwood.*

- *"Richard Branson's balloon came right down on my car and obscured the windscreen."*

- *"An early appearance of the Millennium Bug caused the M25 speed cameras to clock anyone driving faster than 3m.p.h. and I didn't want a ticket."*

- *"I just couldn't be arsed."*

So, as you can see Doug had a certain reputation. After listening to unrelated stories, we would discuss my progress and I would be given a re-write more often than not. Doug would not be available at lunch-times due to his exercise regime especially during the tennis season. The whole thing was painfully slow and I have written my whole life story in a shorter time than that set of notes. However, the notes were eventually completed to Doug's satisfaction and I was ready to get going on my own. That set of notes consisted of 36 pages for the main lesson pre-read, 12 pages for self-assessment test questions and an appendix containing reference material on infectious diseases which had 21 pages. This made a total of 69 pages. Whether these notes are still issued or whether they have been updated, I have no idea, but obviously I still have a copy of the version I wrote!

The T.D.R.U. was situated on the first floor of a building called Farrow House which was on the other side of a train line from the main training school. It was a long office and there were several police personnel and a civilian working there. One Sergeant and a Constable were designated to provide progress tests for the students during their 20-week foundation training course. The Constable, Jim, was a quietly spoken Scotsman who seemed to keep himself to himself. The Sergeant had been in the post for a number of years and was due to be the next victim of the tenure policy. The civilian in the office, Sue (Later to become known as 'my wife at work'), also assisted the exam team.

In the Autumn of 1997, I was called into the Inspector's office and told that I was to replace the Sergeant in the exam team once he left. I was not excited by this prospect as not only had I spent nearly a year learning how to write white notes but I didn't relish the thought of working with Jim, who did not get on with the outgoing Sergeant.

Once I got into how questions were compiled, how exams were supplied to the training school, how they were collected and how they were marked I could see that there needed to be a radical change. Jim was very helpful and we seemed to get on well, especially when I changed the way the exams were delivered. Previously an exam for one intake would be sent by despatch in envelopes for each class and for the appropriate week. This meant that there was no integrity or security and subsequently there would be a difficulty in defending challenges by students. The exam papers were kept in a cupboard and were the same as taken by the previous intake. In many cases there were marks against the answers and also rumours that the order of correct answers sold to the following intake. The course instructors would also go through the questions before sending the papers back. Although it could be said that it was a useful tool for filling in knowledge gaps, it was also a vehicle for the instructors to teach to the test.

Jim and I got into a new system where we would create a new test each time from a bank of questions stored in our computer. The exams were hand delivered on exam day and only sufficient for the number in each class. We also collected the question and answer papers immediately after the exam. This meant that instructors did not see the papers and therefore reduce the chances that they were purely teaching to the test. Jim and I decided that we needed to look at a more reliable system of auto generated exams and marking system and to this end researched who had such systems.

We found out that the Scottish police training school at Tulliallan Castle in Perthshire had a system that sounded good so I asked for permission for me and Jim to visit and investigate. Shortly afterwards we were heading up to Scotland on a train for a few days visit. The turning point in my relationship with Jim was when I suggested that we liven up our coffee purchased on the train, with something from my hip flask. Jim later said, "When you got out that hip flask, I knew that you were the man for me." It was a great trip and we were made very welcome coming away with some good information. Jim, Sue and I made a good team but as we were taking on more work, we needed an extra member of staff to assist with the workload. The boss agreed and an advert placed in police orders. However, I was aware that my old mate Dave with who I had worked so well in the TSU, was working as a gaoler at a nearby police station. I called him and asked him how happy he was there and did he want to come and join us in the exam unit. Having gone through all the correct selection and interview processes, obviously, Dave started with us in January 1999. We worked hard supplying exams not only for the recruit's courses but many other departments. These included, the Detective Training School, the Air Support Unit, Crime Policy Unit, Applied Learning Technology Unit, the Search Wing, Traffic Wardens, Special Constabulary, Area Training Units, Special Intelligence Section, Driving School, Fraud and Finance Faculty and Immigration Enforcement, to name but a few. We had built up a very good reputation for suitable consultation, good communication, incontestable integrity, well-crafted questions and speedy feedback to candidates and supervisors.

I won't go into any detail on each one but a couple stick out in my mind as interesting to mention. We were approached by the Detective Superintendent in charge of the detective foundation course for an exam at the end of their new course. At the initial meeting it was intimated that the need for the exam was to focus the delegates minds on study and stop them just going out on the town at nights (not the actual words used but close enough!). Jim and I challenged this and asked what pass mark they wanted. They misinterpreted our explanation of multiple-choice question marking and against our advice they chose 80%.

We asked for all training material, the aims and objectives for each lesson and set about crafting some questions. We had a panel of trainers who were delivering the course to assess the questions we were writing, all of which were agreed. Come the day of the first exam I took the papers to the exam room to invigilate the exam. At the end I stayed behind to ask the delegates what their feedback on the exam was. That was a big mistake! To say they were not a happy bunch would be an understatement. I very quickly established that our questions did not appear to match up to the delivery and training material as supplied to the students.

After escaping this encounter, I went back to the office to run the answer papers through the marking computer. One of the trainers insisted on being present during the marking process. I told him that this would not be appropriate as we did not want any suspicion of collusion. I ended up locking the doors so that he couldn't get in. I can't remember the number who sat the exam but I do recall that the results showed 13 had failed to attain the required 80%. I took the results to the Detective Superintendent and very shortly afterwards Jim and I were summoned to the conference room in front of him and the instructors.

We were challenged over questions and the process but fought off all matters raised with clear arguments. We reluctantly agreed to go through one particular question that had been poorly answered. After reading it out and giving the options the Detective Chief Inspector told us what he thought the answer should be. We told him that he was correct and he said that the candidates should have got it correct also. In the end and after some considerable time arguing the Detective Superintendent spoke with the Commissioner, Sir Paul Condon, on the phone. After a short conversation it appeared that the Commissioner had backed us and the delegates were told they had failed and would need to take a re-test after a further period of study. Subsequently we received a letter of appreciation from the Detective Superintendent for our work and the way we defended the integrity of the exam. I also received an in-house certificate which read: -

'The Daniel in the Lion's Den Award, is presented to Malcolm Trayhorn for conspicuous and unique bottle when he climbed down the lion's throat on the occasion of the first DC foundation training course final examination 1998'.

We received many letters of appreciation for different projects, which obviously I have kept! We had one from the Detective Chief Inspector in the fraud squad thanking us for help in evaluating and changing questions for the national database received by Association of Chief Police Officers team at Bramshill Police Staff College. We even had one from the then Home Secretary, Jack Straw for the work done in relation to the Immigration Enforcement Pilot Programme.

It was at this time that I thought about shaving off my moustache. My thinking was that growing it in the first place was to make me look older. Perhaps shaving it off would make me look younger? I broached this subject with Barbara one evening and she wasn't keen on the idea as she had never seen me without a moustache and might not like a different look. There was a clever chap in the TDRU who took a photo of my face and then air brushed out the moustache. I took this doctored picture home and showed Barbara. I said, "This is what I might look like without a moustache." She replied, "I suppose it looks OK." I immediately went upstairs and shaved off my 25 years of growth (although not my original growth of course. A bit like Triggers broom really!).

Anyway, I went back downstairs and paraded in front of Barbara. She never noticed the difference and after a while I had to tell her what I had done. I have never grown it back since and looking back at photographs I can't believe that I was allowed to keep it for so long!

Barbara and I were going to be celebrating our 25th Wedding Anniversary On 26th October 1999 and were planning to have a holiday in the Maldives to celebrate. In light of this I took the opportunity of joining the Metropolitan Police Sub Aqua Club, which was affiliated to the British Sub Aqua Club (BSAC). They held their training sessions at Hendon training school swimming pool. In February that year I had a full medical and attended classes to learn all about the equipment and safety procedures. First time wearing the mask, fins, air tanks and buoyancy vest was in the pool. I found it tricky, firstly being able to sink and then being able to stay down at the right depth by either pumping air into the vest or dumping it out. However, eventually I mastered this and even managed to stay upside down at the right depth in the deep end. One skill to get right was to be able to take off your mask, put it back on again and use the air from the mouth piece to expel the water and be able to see again.

On 2nd March we had a trip to Stoney Cove in Leicestershire, to the National Dive Centre in order to practice diving in somewhere other than a swimming pool. This time I was clad in a wet suit and thick gloves as the water was absolutely freezing. In fact, it was so cold that when I lowered myself into the water, it took my breath away and I couldn't breathe let alone put on a mask or mouthpiece. After a few minutes and words of encouragement from the instructor, I managed to get my head under the water and then submerge, letting the weighted belt take me downwards. Once I reached the bottom, I put some air into the buoyancy vest to get me to a depth that allowed me to explore the surrounding area. In the bottom of this pit is an old sunken helicopter so something interesting to look at in a rather bland setting. Once the dive was finished it took some time to get warm again but I had completed the next part of the qualification and just had an open water dive to go. On 19th March I went, with my classmates, to Weymouth Dive Centre, Portland for our open dive part of the BSAC qualification. This time we were to dive in pairs with a compass strapped to our wrists and a line on a reel which was attached to a float, thereby enabling the boat to monitor where we were. Visibility was poor so it was difficult to see anything once underwater. After reaching the correct depth and letting out the rope I suddenly found myself rising to the surface and losing contact with my partner. I quickly dumped all the air from my vest in order to sink down again rapidly but my dive partner was nowhere to be seen. After using my compass to set off in the right direction I remembered that if you became separated from your partner you must surface immediately. When I surfaced, I found my partner and the boat picked us up. Over the next day, we managed to successfully complete our open-water dive and I was now a qualified BSAC diver.

On 17th October 1999 Barbara and I flew out to the Maldives for our holiday and Silver Wedding Anniversary celebration. It was a wonderful holiday but one from which I was lucky to return. I booked some dives for during the two weeks and whilst Barbara lounged in a chair on the beach, I went on my first diving trip in the warm waters of the Indian Ocean. What a difference from Weymouth, no wet suit and beautifully clear water. Just a pair of swimming trunks, a buoyancy vest, fins, mask and air tank. We set off from the shore in a boat, were put into pairs and given a briefing by the diving instructor. When we reached the designated spot, we dropped over the side and slowly descended to approximately 30 metres keeping together as a group as the instructor showed us the sights. The different species of fish, their colours and the coral were absolutely spectacular. I was especially awestruck at the variety of sea life and spotting lobsters peeking out from rocks and small crevices was amazing. What was not quite so amazing was when I was having difficulty breathing. I looked at my air gauge, which I had been keeping an eye on, and it registered that there was 20 Bar of air in the tank. I flippered forward quickly to attract the attention of the instructor but he didn't seem to notice. I was now desperate for air and gave him the signal for, 'I have no air', which is a waving of a flat hand sideways across the throat. He immediately saw that I was in trouble and handed me his spare mouthpiece, attached to his air tank (all tanks had these which are called an octopus). He and myself slowly ascended to 20 metres and stayed at that depth for several minutes before going up to the surface and then on to the boat. The instructor, who was German, was not very happy and asked why I had not noticed my air gauge. I told him that I had checked it and registered me having 20 Bar left. He said that this meant that there was no air left in the tank, something that I failed to fathom! However, I realised how lucky I was that day. Mind you, I did continue to dive a few more times during the holiday. I did not continue when we got home as diving in the cold waters around the U.K. in wet suits, did not appeal to me.

I retired as a serving Police Officer on 9th January 2000 and on 26th January I hired the Bushey Sports Club function room to hold a retirement party. I invited all the people that I had worked with over the years and there were people there from cadet days, my first station, Hoddesdon along with Enfield, Ponders End, Holloway and the Training School as well as members of my family. The first round of drinks cost £189.15 and that was at reduced club prices. The buffet cost £500 but there was no charge for the room as it was a police retirement function. It was a great do with a speech from John, my old Inspector from the TDRU. Traditionally the speech would be given by your current senior officer but as he wasn't invited and John was more of a friend, he gave the address. John's wife, also a serving police officer, later asked me to do a speech at his retirement do which I did in my traditional poem style. I wrote and delivered many such poem style speeches over time at different functions and have copies of most of them. Anyway, at my do, I was presented with a tankard (surprised?)

The inscription read: -

Malcolm on your retirement 9th JAN 2000.

I also received a magnificent circular barometer which has an inscription in the centre: -

SERGEANT 920CO MALCOLM TRAYHORN

And round the inside edge that reads: -

Presented To Police Sergeant Malcolm Trayhorn By His Friends & Colleagues On His Retirement From The Metropolitan Police On 9th January 2000.

Chapter 19 – Executive Officer

In late 1999 I had given notice that I intended to take my retirement, having completed 30 years pensionable service. Nobody really took much notice until I put in my official resignation letter and then there was a realisation that there had been no succession planning to find a replacement for what was a specialist post. I was asked if I would stay on as a civilian to do the same job upon my retirement date. Subsequently an advert was placed in police notices asking for applicants, as required. I applied for the post and guess what? I got the job. So, I retired as a uniformed police Sergeant on the 9th January 2000 and started as a suited and booted civilian Grade 10 Executive Officer on 10th January 2000.

That was a very emotive moment for me even though I would be doing the same job I had spent 32 years as a police officer and that had come to an end. Did I get a word of thanks from senior management or the personnel manager saying thanks for your valued service and dedication plus a welcome to the civilian branch of the service? The answer to that question was a resounding NO! I was not surprised.

However, I still had a job that I enjoyed working with Jim, Dave and Sue, so I just shrugged it off and got on with the work of the exam unit. Over the next few months things started to change in respect of attitudes and a dulling down of the standards relating to exams. I got the impression that senior management did not take kindly to a civilian advising them and asking for more help to fulfil requirements being placed on the unit. Things came to a head when I discovered that another retiring police officer had been taken on at a higher rate of pay for performing a similar role. I put in a grievance under the grievance procedure which covered lack of support plus inequality. A Chief Inspector attempted to resolve the matter but I felt did not address the issue so I asked for the grievance to be taken to the next stage. A Superintendent initially tried to placate me by saying that the matter could be sorted out reasonably as responsible adults. That was fine by me until I found out through reliable sources (I had friends on the inside) that this Superintendent set up meetings where he was looking to effectively chop my legs. The Chief Inspector spoke to me about how things were progressing and I said, "Don't speak to me, I think you are in a conspiracy with the Superintendent to chop my legs." She said, "No absolutely not." I informed her that I knew about the meetings that had taken place to discredit me. She went to see the Superintendent and when she came back, she said, "I'm very sorry Malcolm it looks like you were right." Needless to say, I requested the grievance to go to stage 3, much to the annoyance of the Superintendent. On 10th October 2000 I ended up in front of the Commander who couldn't have been nicer. He said that as far as the exam situation was concerned and the suggestion that it should be better supported, "We would like a Rolls Royce but we have to settle for a Ford Mondeo." I said, "Well you have got Del and Rodney's three wheeled van and one of the wheels has come off." The upshot was that he didn't see how any parts of my grievance could be resolved to my satisfaction and it was sad that a 30 plus year career should end in this way. I said that I no longer wanted my name associated with the exam unit and felt that my integrity was worth more to me. I therefore resigned from the Metropolitan Police on the 17th October 2000.

Before leaving I had an exit interview with the personnel manager where I told her exactly what I thought about my treatment and her lack of interest in her staff, in particular. I had not had any recognition or thanks for my 32 years police service (this comment was directed at senior police managers), no welcome to the civilian branch of the service or any support (this comment was directed at her). I was glad to get that off my chest so that I could move on.

And the lesson today

Pass-Out Day picture

Pay attention class

172

Leading Pass-out Parade

The Greenies

Taking the Salute

Interview

Sir Peter Imbert Reviewing Officer

Charity walk team

Bloodmobile Gang

Cross Country with Recruits

Finishing '94 London Marathon

In Training

Winning Pike Fishing Trophy

Greenies Yachting Club

Open Water Dive

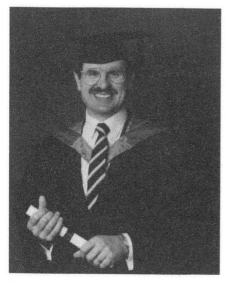

Graduation Day

ERIC RICHARD
as SGT. BOB CRYER

FROM THAMES TV'S
THE BILL

Area Training

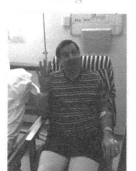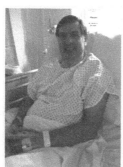

New Hip

With Dad

Dave, Me, Jim

Exam Team Get Together

With Maureen

Steve's Caricature

Long Service & Good Conduct

Chapter 20 – Bloodmobile

As I knew that I would be resigning I was looking round for something new to do. I had been a blood donor since I was 19 and on a visit to my local session around this time, I saw that they were looking for staff. I spoke to the ladies about the position and got an application form. As a consequence, I subsequently started as a Donor Carer for the National Blood Service on 23rd October 2000. I was attached to a mobile unit that toured all over the region setting up at factories, large companies, police headquarters and supermarket car parks. Someone would drive the lorry and trailer to the venue and we would travel to meet it in a mini bus. The trailer had extendable sides and was large enough to accommodate a reception area, a health-check test area, 6 beds, a pack checking area and some seats for dishing out refreshments at the end.

Initially I was doing the reception role on the computer progressing to the healthcare questionnaires, blood prick testing, pack checking and occasionally tea making. I was soon check tested on the minibus and became the driver backwards and forwards to the home base at Colindale, just round the corner from Hendon. I never got round to being trained to put needles into people's arms but did spend many times looking after donors during blood giving and then filling test tubes with samples for checking and taking needles out. The majority of staff on these units were women and many of them had been with the blood service for many years. What a lovely bunch of people they were and I made some really good friends in the short time I spent with them. One lady, Maureen, always called me, 'my Malcolm' and would give me a cuddle when she saw me. The shifts were 12 hours and the pay wasn't great but the company was and the work very rewarding. The manager of the bloodmobile approached me on one occasion and asked me if I would be the trainer for the team as I was a qualified trainer. I asked him what my extra remuneration would be for this and when he said there would be no extra money, I told him NO.

During my time with the blood service I attended the retirement do of one of my old work colleagues from our Farrow House days. During the evening one of the guys still working there approached me and asked me if I might be interested in working at the communications school at Farrow House as a trainer. He said that his boss had asked him to speak to me and see if I would go back as a trainer for a new programme as they were desperate for experienced trainers. I was not sure about this but said I might be interested. The next day I had a call from the boss of the communications school offering me a well-paid job as a trainer with regular hours and weekends off. I said that this would suit me nicely and she said that she would sort things out with personnel and get me in-post as soon as possible. A short time later that day she called me back to say that she was very sorry and embarrassed to tell me that she had spoken to the personnel manager who said, *"We're not having him back"*. This was a lesson to me that one should never burn one's bridges!

Chapter 21 – Back to Stanborough

However, fate played a hand yet again that year as a friend told me that Hertfordshire Constabulary were desperately seeking experienced trainers at their Headquarters training department at Stanborough, Welwyn Garden City. I gave them a call and shortly thereafter visited the Inspector in charge to discuss the position on offer. I was required to attend for a formal interview and also to give a lesson to a group of their current staff. It was a bit like Deja-vu going back to teach in a classroom where I was a student cadet back in 1968, some 33 years previously. I was offered the job and so left the Blood Service to begin a new role as a civilian trainer for Hertfordshire Constabulary on 30th July 2001. On my first day I was shown my desk in the staff room and I noticed a uniform jacket on the back of a chair on the next desk. What drew my attention to it was that it had the number 844 on the shoulder, which was my number when I was a PC in Herts. from 1970 to 1974. When the owner of the tunic, Peter, came back I introduced myself and asked him how long he had had the number 844 and if he knew who had it before him. He said that he had got the number when he joined back in 1975 but didn't know who had it before him. I told him that I did know who it was and that it was me. His face was a picture and we never tired of telling the story.

I was involved in many courses over the next two years at the training department including those for: – recruits foundation, probationers' continuation, Sergeant's promotion, diversity, policing styles, communication operations and switchboard operators. I got on well with all the police and civilian trainers there and also the head of training. However, there was a change of Sergeant when the delightful Sue retired and I did not have much respect for her replacement. The recruit foundation course was a two-week introduction to the police service and preparation for their 13-week course at District Training School. I was involved in 7 of these courses during my time at Herts as a civilian trainer involving over 200 recruits. I found these courses most enjoyable and attended the attestation ceremonies for all of these. I also delivered numerous continuation training courses for those probationers who had returned from training school and had to attend H.Q. during their two-year probationary period.

The Constabulary, at this time engaged an outside agency to deliver diversity training across all members working for them. In order to give a police perspective to the content of the inputs, a Herts trainer assisted at each of the sessions. Due to my experience and Home Office approved qualification in this area I was involved with them in these sessions. This meant travelling around the county and meeting a mixture of constabulary members from senior officers to traffic wardens to admin support personnel and community support officers. This was one of my most challenging experiences as a trainer.

On Friday 10th May 2002 a train was derailed at Potters Bar railway station. As soon as the news broke that there were a number of deaths and injuries a casualty bureau was set up at H.Q. to deal with calls from concerned members of the public. Together with others I was requested to join the team answering the phone calls being made by concerned relatives. We were just obtaining details of the caller and who they were concerned about. Further down the line any that matched up with injured or fatalities would be contacted either in person or by phone depending on the circumstances. There were 7 deaths as a result of this incident. All of us involved in helping in the Casualty Bureau for this incident received a letter of thanks from the Assistant Chief Constable.

On one occasion they were short of training staff so employed someone from an agency to fill the shortfall for a time. Dennis, who came, was a retired Detective Sergeant from Greater Manchester Police who lived in Cheshire. The agency who placed him, put him up in a local hotel during the week. I quickly became great friends with him and invited him to our house one evening for a home cooked meal of Barbara's steak and kidney pie. Dennis never stopped talking about it for years afterwards and in fact still does. I was invited to his daughter's wedding and I was to be able to offer him work later. One thing he did for me was to persuade me to join an agency. I wasn't sure about this as I was getting a regular salary and able to go home every night. However, he pointed out that I was on poor wages as a civilian employee of the constabulary and had to abide by all the internal politics, whereas all he did was to arrive, deliver the training and leave. He was also on a very competitive daily fee, well above what I was receiving and worth the inconvenience of working away from home during the week.

Chapter 22 – Agency Work

I spoke to a couple of agencies, one of which offered me a two-week contract to deliver training at £150 per day. I said that I would be interested and let the head of training know what I was intending to do. She said that she would be sorry to see me leave, understood why I had made the decision but would happily have me back should things not work out with the agency. In the meantime, I was contacted by another agency who offered me two weeks work at Thames Valley police training headquarters at the White House, Sulhamstead, Berkshire. The deal was for a fee of £200 per day plus accommodation and food. This was the contract I accepted and although it was only for two weeks and an uncertainty as to whether I would get any other work thereafter, I bit the bullet and went for it. The agency was in London and they had a database of retired police personnel who they could call upon to supply to forces around the country for all manner of roles. This is the National Retired Officers Database (NROD) of which I became a member.

I started at Sulhamstead on 26th August 2003 and slotted right in, together with their own staff and other agency trainers. There was Derby from a Northern force, Nigel from a Southern force and Bruce from Sussex, all retired officers. I was delivering a continuation course for the two weeks and received good feedback from the students that led to me being offered an extension to my contract. I was to stay at Thames Valley delivering a variety of training courses for the next 13 months. I got to be part of the furniture and even had my own set of rooms in the upper floor of a house which was used as a rape suite on the ground floor.

During the probationers training courses and whilst at the centre, they had to undergo their fitness tests. This consisted of an endurance running element, known as the bleep test and some strength exercises. Although, as a civilian, I was not expected to take part in these, I always joined them, in order to hold credibility and acceptance with each group. The bleep test was done on the tennis court with lines marked out at each end, fifteen meters apart. It started with a long gap between each bleep so that you could walk to the other end of the tennis court and touch the line with your foot before the bleep sounded. You would turn round and head back to the other line before the next bleep. The gap between bleeps got less and less so that you would have to get faster and faster in order to keep up. The probationers were expected to get to a certain level in order to pass this test (level 5.4 with only 6 seconds between bleeps). The idea was to keep going as long as you could and it was always a competition to see who had the best stamina and fitness. The majority did pass the test and I am proud to say I also reached the standard and in fact beat over half of them each time I did it. I might add that I was now in my 50's and most of them in their 20's.

When this came to an end the agency secured me a contract with British Transport training centre at Tadworth in Surrey. This time I was put up in a hotel a short distance away. That was in early January of 2005 and I was delivering probationer continuation training courses there. Another assignment with the Transport Police was to assist a local trainer in training Police Community Support Officers (PCSO's). This was at premises right next to the Tower of London. I met the lead trainer for the course on the first morning and asked what the timetable for the two-week course was. He showed me a rough guide as to what he wanted covered but when I asked for any lesson plans, aims and objectives or equipment he told me that there wasn't any. I was surprised at the lack of planning or guidance for a visiting agency trainer. I made the mistake of saying to him that I would cover as much as he wanted me to over the two weeks. He said that he had work to do back at his office so would leave me to start the course. I never saw him for the rest of the two weeks and put together the course content myself. I have to say that the quality of the students was not the best, although some of the class of 16 were keen. I finished the course and the Transport Police trainer was very happy with the results. There was one student who was a bit of a nightmare over the duration of the course and I had to reprimand him more than once for his behaviour and improper responses. When I checked in with the lead trainer some weeks later, he told me that this individual had been arrested for theft just after the course. At least he knew what the offence of theft was, or at least he had been at a lesson explaining it!

I was with British Transport Police and also back with Thames Valley at Sulhamstead up until June of 2005. I then contacted the agency and asked if they had any more work for me. They told me that British Transport Police wanted me back but they were looking to set up their own training section and were looking for a training manager. Amongst others on their books apparently my name had come up as being suitable for the role and asked if I was interested. I told them that I wasn't really as I preferred to be in front of a class teaching.

Shortly after I had a call from Miles, a director of the agency who persuaded me to visit their offices in London to discuss the proposal. On 20th June that year I attended their offices in Whitcomb Street, London, situated just behind Leicester Square. I met Miles, a director plus another person whose name was Tony, a retired Assistant Chief Constable. Together they were looking to deliver training courses by experienced and qualified detectives to police forces and other bodies around the country. The role sounded interesting and I asked what the next stage would be. They wanted me to attend for a formal interview and give a presentation as to how I saw the role. I attended the offices on 30th June and gave a presentation before being questioned by three people (Miles, the director, Tony, the retired Assistant Chief Constable and a retired Detective Superintendent). The interview was one of the most challenging I had ever had to endure and was convinced that I had no chance of getting the post. I have no idea how many others were up for interview or short-listed for the job but on 11th July 2005, after being offered the position and accepting, I started as a training development manager for the agency. This meant that my training delivery days were at an end and there were to be no more captive audiences to perform to (I mean teach!) I kept an electronic file for each of the subject areas that I had taught over my years of training delivery and when I counted how many there were it came to 102 files with lesson plans and material relating to each subject.

The first project I was given was to organise a seminar on Elder Abuse at a Hotel. This was all new to me so I might have been a bit slow on the uptake at times. This might have been evident as I was summoned into the conference room at the London Office one day and challenged on details of where the project was up to and costings. Tony was never one to suffer fools gladly and when he wanted something done, he wanted it done directly, correctly and effectively. He asked me for something that I wasn't able to give in relation to costings and said, "Mr Trayhorn I've asked you twice for this now, I suggest that you go back to your desk and sort it out." Although I wasn't fazed by his outburst, Miles must have thought that he had been a bit strong because a few minutes later Tony came out of the conference room and over to my desk to see if I was alright. Although a tough and demanding task master I managed to hold on to the training development manager job for five years. During that time, I was involved in the organisation of numerous training courses around the country, mainly to senior detectives and investigators.

I had the pleasure of meeting and working with some very experienced and interesting senior detectives, most of them recently retired. Some of the courses were: – 'Serious Crime Investigation Review Training', 'Death in Custody', Advanced Road Death Investigation, 'Initial Crime Investigators Development Programme', 'Regulation of Investigatory Powers Act 2000', 'Professional Standards Investigation Course', 'Professionalising the Investigation Programme', 'Major Incident Room Training' and 'Corporate Manslaughter', to name but a few. My job was to ensure that all the speakers were contracted, their terms of reference drawn up, any transport and accommodation arranged for them, training venues identified and secured plus draw up service level agreements for any force or body for whom we were providing the training. I was also responsible for the collation and printing of all course documents, of which there were a lot. I think my role description also stated that I had to perform any other duties and functions requested by the directors (i.e. general dog's body!)

The office in London was an open plan affair with different sections. There was the police section, for the recruitment and placing of retired officers, the medical section, which was for the recruitment and placement of medical personnel and the education section for the recruitment and placing of educational personnel. I got on well with everyone in the office and would bring packets of chocolate biscuits each week to put in the tea room for all. It was decided that a head of training was needed to further the possibilities of the training side, so the post was advertised. I was asked about this and said that I felt that I was not the right person for this and preferred to stick with the organising side of things. One of the applicants was a retiring Detective Superintendent who I had previously met at the Detective Training School at Hendon, then a Detective Chief Inspector. His name was also Tony and not that my opinion counted for much, I suggested that he would be ideal for the role. Shortly after he was taken on and therefore, I had another boss to work for.

Things within the company changed during these years and instead of being a Limited Company it was changed to a Public Limited Company so that it could offer shares in the company to the public. The company changed its name but in order to remain visible to our clients we kept some of our previous name. Over the five years several ideas about location for a dedicated office were explored. For a short time, there was an office in Southampton before another was established in Micheldever near Winchester. This proved to be unsuitable and so other premises were found nearby, still in Micheldever. Another followed in Portsmouth and eventually one in Derby. This one was purpose built for us with offices and classrooms so that we could run courses on site. Due to my involvement in courses it was necessary to attend the offices on a fairly regular basis, so I was frequently on the road, especially down to Micheldever and Portsmouth plus up to Derby. To make it worthwhile I stayed overnight in a local Hotels or Bed and Breakfasts in a local pub. As I arranged the training venues, I was always looking at conference and hotel facilities, visiting them and negotiating the best deals. I got to know many contacts during those years and when I attended any of the courses and stayed overnight, I always got the best rooms.

Some of the people we engaged to deliver the course content were experienced in teaching but some, although experts in their field, were not the best at delivery. There was one retired Detective Superintendent, who was a bit dry with his delivery and his sessions not the liveliest. After assessing a lesson one day I did say to him that I was going to have to teach him to tap-dance. Luckily, he saw the funny side and took the advice in the spirit it was given.

Because it was essential to have evidence of the quality of the courses it was decided to work towards a recognised award. For the style of courses being delivered it was decided that we should endeavour to get the Skills for Justice, 'Skillsmark' award. Together with Ian, a work colleague at the agency and someone I had worked with at Hendon, I began the process of putting together evidence. We compiled a quality manual and all the other documentation required to fulfil the criteria for the award. Ian and I spent many hours and days on this application but this paid off as, after many months work and re-writes we became one of a very few private training providers who achieved the "Skillsmark" award.

The agency had a quality assurance award with the International Organisation for Standardisation (ISO) which required each section of the company to have Quality Manual setting out procedures and standards. I had responsibility for putting all this together and maintaining it for our section and managed to pass two annual inspections. The ISO badge was recognised by clients to signify that you were a company fit to deal with and had proper quality systems in place. It was therefore very useful to have.

I remember going to the London offices of the Independent Police Complaints Commission (IPCC), who wanted some training for their operational investigators in health and safety issues when attending incidents. I engaged a recommended qualified trainer, with credentials in health and safety. The one-day course was agreed and a date set for delivery. As the trainer was not someone I knew and had not been assessed by me I decided to attend the first delivery to do an assessment. It was clear from the outset that the person was not suitable and, in my opinion, a dreadful trainer. At the end of the day I asked him to wait in the reception area whilst I spoke to the IPCC representative who had been present during the day and was obviously not impressed. I apologised for the sub-standard level of delivery and said that we would change the trainer forthwith. I then gave the so-called trainer feedback on his delivery, thanked him but told him that we would not be using him in the future. I contacted Frank, a trainer I knew from my police days who was a trainer and also conversant with health and safety. He took over delivery of this course and the feedback was very positive. The contract was therefore saved and we went on to deliver further training to the IPCC.

This was not the only trainer whose services I dispensed with. Tony made a contact with someone at the Food Standards Agency who was responsible for organising courses for their investigators. We attended their offices in London and spoke to Bob, the contact there who said that he was happy with the trainer they had been using, but might be looking for a different company to deal with. I managed to track down and get in touch with the trainer they had delivering for the other company and he was agreeable to deliver the training through us. He came down from Liverpool to our offices in London and he talked a very good job, so with him on board we managed to secure the contract. As before I attended the first delivery to assess the trainer and was not impressed with his abilities. I spoke with Bob, the Food Standards Agency contact, who was more than happy with the course content and delivery. However, I told him that although he thought that trainer was good, we could do a lot better.

I contacted my old mate Dennis (from Herts days) and got him on board to deliver this course. Subsequently, Dennis ended up delivering this course for the FSA around the country and the man at the FSA said YES! When Dennis was not available to deliver the course, I engaged Bruce, another old mate from Thames Valley days. He then became the FSA contact's favourite trainer. Something I believed was key to the success of a course was, 'Know thy trainer'! This course was delivered to many Food Standards Agency investigators throughout England, Scotland and Wales.

One of the more challenging contracts to secure was for the Office of the Police Ombudsman for Northern Ireland (OPONI) for their staff investigating complaints against the police. After submitting a tender bid, we were shortlisted to deliver the training programme. Ian and I flew over to Belfast to be interviewed by their panel of senior personnel. We came out of their conference room a bit shell shocked and certainly had a grilling. To our surprise they did engage our agency to deliver their training. I engaged a lead trainer to oversee this complex accredited investigative training programme together with supporting trainers.

In 2007 it was decided by Tony and the company directors that we would host the National Police Training managers conference. Of course, that meant that I would secure the venue for this and having run courses there, I booked a hotel conference facility near Rugby. There was a lot of organising for this event, which attracted training managers and key speakers from police forces all over the country. At this event there was to be an award for the training manager of the year, decided by a panel consisting of eminent people at the Home Office and Her Majesty's Inspector of Constabulary (HMIC). As our agency was hosting the event, it was decided that a representative from the company should be on the panel. I was delegated by Tony to perform this task, so I attended the London Offices of HMIC to join the great and good in selecting the winning training manager from evidence and testimonials submitted. Coincidentally and quite deservedly, the person selected was my old boss at Hertfordshire Constabulary, who had said that she would have me back any time.

I can't remember how we got the contact with Cardiff Harbour but I ended up travelling there on 13th February 2008 to discuss with them a training programme for their wardens in enforcing new by-laws plus gathering and securing evidence. I engaged Frank (of the IPCC course) to deliver this training, which he and I put together with all presentations and supporting material for three two-day courses. This was well received and got good feedback.

Tony got us a contact with the Home Office, who were looking for someone to put together and deliver a Licensing Enforcement Programme. I attended the Home Office on several occasions to discuss requirements and update our contact with progress. The walk from our offices in Whitcomb Street to Marsham Street was just over a mile but on a nice day was very pleasant and took in some of the sights. First a stroll past the National Gallery and along the side of Trafalgar Square passing Admiralty Arch and crossing the Mall with views up to Buckingham Palace. Then into Horse Guards Road passing Horse Guards Parade and the Imperial War Museum, Churchills War Rooms. Across Birdcage Walk and into Storeys Gate passing Central Hall

Westminster then across Victoria Street into Great Smith Street, passing Westminster Abbey on the left. This eventually led into Marsham Street where the Home Office is situated.

One of the things they wanted was a supporting CD and booklet with guidance and advice. I engaged another old friend from Hendon days, Leigh (who had been my Inspector in the TSU) and had the relevant skills. Subsequently I engaged a retired police trainer with an expertise in licensing legislation and enforcement. The contract was to deliver 50 seminars around the country, including administrative responsibilities and a Website. Although not all, I did attend several of these seminars to ensure everything was in place at the venues and things ran smoothly. The publication that was produced fully explained licensing law and Home Office guidance supporting the seminars and complimenting the CD. It has an acknowledgement at the back to all those who were involved of which my name was one.

Chapter 23 – A New Company & 'Four Old Gits in a Boat'

In 2009 a new Executive Officer took over the reins of the company and a decision was made that they would return to just recruitment as they said they were losing money. Tony (the ex-Detective Superintendent) saw the writing on the wall and so decided to leave, but as I had a six-month notice agreement, I was kept on to see out the Home Office contract and other training that we were still contracted to deliver.

Towards the end of 2009 Tony decided that he would set up his own training company in conjunction with three other retired Detective Superintendents. I was invited along to an early meeting of this group in a public house in London. I was told that a sign of the company taking off would be if they were able to take me on as their training development manager. Some weeks passed and on 2nd March 2010 I received a call from Tony saying that we needed to have a conversation. As a result, I was offered the role of training manager for the newly formed training company. My role was pretty much the same as I had performed at the agency and many of the same courses were to be delivered using the same trainers. My worth was largely due to the data base I had collected of trainers with all their CV's, contact details and the fact that senior officers, albeit retired, were used to delegating jobs and not doing them themselves. More than once I was told, "It's our job to get the clients and then it's your job to keep them."

Not long after I began working for them, one of the directors and founder members left the company leaving three. I was not involved in this, obviously, but I do know that it was not an amicable parting of the ways. Later down the line there was another rift when one director did not see eye to eye with the other two, so he also left. That was a shame as far as I was concerned because I always got on with him and liked him. Then there were two!

191

Other Courses that I was involved in progressing and providing support and administration for included, Accountable Officer training in England, Scotland and Wales, Serious Crime Investigating for detectives in Bahrain, organising and sourcing various training courses for the Royal Air Force Military Police, Court Security Officers training programme in conjunction with Amey plc and the Certificate in Knowledge of Policing. These are a few of the thirty plus courses and projects that I was involved with during my time with the company. Apart from preparing all contracts, printing all documents, engaging trainers, finding and booking venues, assessing trainers, visiting courses and attending board meetings, I distributed, collected, analysed and implemented any changes that were identified from end of course questionnaires

The Certificate in the Knowledge of Policing or CKP was a training programme sanctioned by the College of Policing for anyone wishing to join the police. In order to apply for a position with a police force, an applicant would first have to pass an academic qualification that they have taken at their own cost. In order to become a preferred provider of this training programme any provider had to satisfy the College of Policing that the standards, trainers and programme satisfied their criteria. This was a huge undertaking and gathering all the material, setting all lesson aims and objectives, formulating exam questions, sourcing suitable delivery venues and engaging suitably qualified trainers were just a part of this project. I had to find suitable premises around London that could accommodate classes of students at weekends at a reasonable cost. I found and agreed contracts with Westminster Kingsway College, Jurys Inn Hotel in Croydon, Greenwich Naval College and Kings College in The Strand. I was backwards and forwards to London quite a lot during this period, briefing students, assessing trainers and overseeing exams.

Another challenging contract was to facilitate training courses for the Ministry of Defence and the Royal Airforce Military Police specifically. This contract was obtained in conjunction with a company called Bond Solon and required me to find courses being run by police forces around the country and secure places on them for RAF personnel. This was wide ranging and included drug awareness, advanced driving, advanced source handling and sexual offences investigation trained officer to name but a few.

Apart from all the visits to venues and attending various meetings with the directors I was able to do most of the organising and printing from home. I set up a spare bedroom as an office and took over responsibility for all the printing of course material and supporting documents as the director's wife who was doing this said that she no longer wanted to continue with this time-consuming job. I was regularly at the local Staples store collecting boxes of paper, ring binders, section dividers and other stationary items. After I had done the printing for a course, collated the printed pages and put them in the relevant sections in the ring binders I was down my local post office regularly with boxes full of printed files to be delivered to training venues. I also had to arrange couriers to deliver supporting training equipment such as laptop computer, projector and all electrical leads. If I was visiting a course, I would take some with me to the venue.

As I was spending a lot of time working in the spare bedroom/office I did allow myself a break a couple of times a week to spend a couple of hours at the local gym. This was a private members club attached to a golf course and had a small gym set up together with a sauna, steam room, jacuzzi and a pool. I would spend an hour in the gym then relax in the pool area followed by a swim and a steam plus jacuzzi. On one such occasion (it was on 29th November 2010, a day I will never forget). I had left Barbara at home in bed with a bad migraine. I went to the gym and having completed my gym workout, was having a leisurely swim in the pool. I started to feel unwell and decided to get out of the pool. As I did so I started to get the most excruciating pain in my chest and had to curl up at the side of the pool clutching my chest. One of the regulars, Giuseppe, saw that I was in difficulty and came over to me. He asked me if I needed any help and I said, "Yes, I think I do".

Giuseppe raised the alarm and in no time, there were staff from the gym trying to calm me down and assist. I have to say that although conscious and mindful of people around me, I was in so much pain that I was fairly oblivious to a lot of it. The next thing I knew there was a paramedic spraying something under my tongue. I found out later that this was Glyceryl trinitrate (GTN), a spray used to relieve chest pain.

When sprayed under the tongue, it relaxes and widens blood vessels in the heart and the rest of the body to try and open them up. I found that the pain did subside slightly as I was removed to an ambulance and driven to the QE II Hospital Casualty Department in Welwyn Garden City. During the journey the pain intensified again in my chest and I was unable to stop shaking and clutching my chest. Upon arrival at the Hospital I was immediately put on an Electrocardiogram (ECG) and I heard the sister saying, "Try to calm down Mr Trayhorn so that we can get a proper reading." Easy for her to say! She was very matter-of-fact I thought asking who was at home and what was the phone number. I said, "My wife, but don't ring her because she is in bed with a migraine." "You're having a heart attack Mr Trayhorn we have to contact someone."

So, I was having a heart attack? The thought had not entered my mind, although to be fair nothing had entered my mind, only knowing that I was in pain. I heard the sister say, "This man needs to get to the Lister as soon as possible, he hasn't got much time." I was just beginning to realise that I was in serious trouble. The ambulance crew that conveyed me to the Hospital from the gym, loaded me back into the ambulance and we were off to the Lister Hospital in Stevenage. I was always given to understand that in order to keep a casualty calm the use of audible warning equipment and excessive speed were kept to a minimum. That was out of the window and I was being thrown around in the back whilst the driver went hell-for-leather during the thirteen-mile journey with full bells and whistles blaring out.

When we arrived, I was wheeled on the stretcher, still in my wet swimming shorts, into the operating room, where they were awaiting my arrival. I remember a doctor speaking to me and saying that he needed to point out the risks of the operation and that I needed to sign the consent form. He said, "Of course the decision is yours but if you don't have it you will die." Oh! What a decision! It won't surprise you to know that I signed the form, albeit in very shaky handwriting. Next thing I was lying flat on my back on the operating table with my right arm outstretched with a sheet covering from the elbow downwards so that I couldn't see what was going on. I was expecting to be sedated so I was not conscious but that wasn't the case. A large Xray type machine was manoeuvred over my chest area and I was asked to move my head either left or right depending on where they wanted to move the monitor.

After a while, I have no idea how long it was but it didn't seem like long at all, he said, "That's it, all done." He showed me two monitor screens with pictures of my heart and surrounding vessels before the operation and another showing the same area after the operation. I could clearly see that there was little or no sign of blood flowing through the vessels on the before picture but full flow in the after picture. He told me that they had inserted a wire through my wrist which they were able to manipulate through a vessel until it reached the blocked artery in my heart. With the incredible technology of this equipment they pushed through the blockage, dispersing it and then left a small mesh called a stent, which was pushed into place by opening it out using a small balloon and leaving it there. This procedure is called an angioplasty. I was then wheeled into another room to recuperate. By this time, I was sitting up and feeling fine. The nurse asked me if I would like a cup of tea, which I readily accepted and asked if I could have my phone to call Barbara to put her mind to rest. I got through to her and she said she was on the way to the hospital but couldn't talk. When she arrived, I was sitting up, drinking tea and feeling well. She said that she had had a rude awakening when the Sister from Welwyn Garden City Hospital rang her. Apparently, she said, "I don't want to worry you Mrs Trayhorn but your husband is having a heart attack." Of course, you realise after such an episode how precious life is and how trivial things don't matter. I treasure each day from that day until this.

I thought that the pain I experienced with the heart attack was bad enough but on 1st July 2011, I was to experience another very significant painful experience. I was suffering initially from a back ache but during the day and into the evening it got worse and moved to my groin. By the early hours of the morning of 2nd July I was doubled over in agony and reluctantly I accepted that I needed to get to hospital. Barbara drove me to the casualty department at Harlow where I was eventually seen by a doctor. It was suspected that I might have a grumbling appendix or a hernia but an x-ray did not confirm this. I was admitted into a ward so that I could have a CT scan the following day. I was given strong pain killers, which didn't seem to help much and lay in bed waiting for what seemed like an eternity. When they eventually took me for a scan, I was in so much pain that I was unable to lie still on my back long enough for the scan to be successful. I was let know that they were not very happy that I was unable to remain still long enough as these scans are very costly (easy for them to say). I was taken back to the ward and given more pain killers until a second try was made the following day. This time I was assigned a dedicated pain nurse who pumped me with morphine and pain killer tablets.

Although still in agony I did manage to get through the scan procedure. The following morning the doctor, on his rounds came to me and said, "So it was a slipped disc then?" I said, "Was it, no one told me." I was released from the hospital on Monday 11th July, nine days after being admitted. I got no treatment for this, only bed rest and pain relief. In a follow up outpatient visit I was told that it was a common complaint in people of my age owing to the deterioration of the discs and any strain causing one to pop out and trap nerves. So that was two episodes within a year, I couldn't say which was the most painful but each of them was extremely so at the time they happened.

Over the years my friendship with Fred and Colin continued, mainly via the phone and cards at Christmas and Birthdays. Colin and his wife Jan only lived a few miles from our house so I would pop round to see them every now and then. Fred had divorced from Gillikins and gone back to his native Scotland; in fact, he had a flat that overlooked the cricket pitch that we had camped on years before. Fred had visited us now and again, when he was down from Scotland to visit his children. In July of 2011 Colin and I boarded a train up to Glasgow in order to have an old boy's reunion. Fred's adopted brother, 'Wee Ian', picked us up in his taxi and took us to Fred's flat in Paisley. The name, 'Wee Ian' dated back to when Fred got married and Ian was a very small young lad. He could certainly not be described as wee any more but his name stuck and he will always be 'Wee Ian'.

The plan was to meet up with a mate of Fred's who he regularly went sailing with, from Inverkip, a small village some fifteen miles away on the edge of the Firth of Clyde. John, was of a similar age to the three of us and we made an instant connection. As it was John's yacht he was referred to as, 'Captain John'. The yacht was only a small affair and just big enough for the four of us. So, after loading our gear and provisions, we set off along the Clyde. Our expeditions could form a book of its own and would be called, 'Four old Gits in a boat.' Captain John said that he loved listening to the three of us reminiscing about our times in the police, especially our exploits when stationed together at Hoddesdon.

We stopped overnight at Port Bannatyne and the next day sailed to Portavadie, where we stayed overnight. On the way the weather was not the best, with some rain and a fair bit of wind. We had water proof clothing on as well as lifejackets. I was wearing my favourite baseball cap which unfortunately was blown off in a sudden gust whilst turning the boat. It went drifting off down the Clyde, never to be seen again! Colin bought me a new baseball cap when we were at the next port and from then on, I had a piece of string attached to my clothing and a peg on the other end, which was clipped to the cap. It was a great trip and we vowed to do it again.

Before returning home, Fred took us to the Brig o' Doon House Hotel, a posh Hotel in Ayr for a final meal. I had a liking for sticky toffee pudding with lashings of toffee sauce and hot custard and as they had it on their menu, I ordered it. Fred and Colin always exaggerate the sticky toffee pudding episode but if something you're paying good money for isn't right and they ask you, then you have to tell them, don't you? When ordering I asked the young waitress if it was a proper sticky toffee pudding with dates and if the custard was going to be hot, she assured me it was and would be. The girl waitress turned up with a pudding but was really more like a steamed chocolate sponge pudding. It looked OK but no hint of dates and then produced a jug with an insipid looking cold liquid. I said, "I did ask if the custard would be hot and this isn't custard and certainly not hot." "Sorry sir, that is crème anglaise." I now constantly get reminded of the incident with untrue tales that I made the poor waitress cry and that she had said, "Well it was hot when I left the kitchen." Now, if we are out and there is sticky toffee pudding on the menu the first comment is, "Does it come with hot custard?"

Colin and I did travel back up to Scotland the following year and we set off with Captain John on 29th July for, "Four old Gits in a boat," part deux. This time we sailed to Millport where we stayed overnight in the Cathedral of the Isles, which is Britain's smallest Cathedral and dates from 1851. The next day we sailed to Lochranza on the Isle of Arron and booked into the Castlekirk Arthouse bed and breakfast. That night we had a tremendous meal in the famous Stag's Pavilion restaurant nearby. The next day we paid a visit to the famous Arron distillery where we sampled the whisky and purchased a few bottles between us. After another day on Arron we sailed back to Inverkip where Captain John cooked us a Chilli at his riverside residence. As it was a Thursday it coincided with Fred's cinema club night, so we went with a chum of Fred's to the pictures. We saw 'Ted', which was about a teddy bear that comes to life and behaves just like an irresponsible adult. It would be an understatement to say that Colin was not amused. The next day we walked round to Lillian's house, Fred's sister and drove to Loch Lomond for lunch at the Boat House restaurant at Cameron House. Another successful trip and sadly the last we would be taking together.

Episode three of the medical issues, was not in the same league as the other two but still a significant event in the health stakes. I had been getting a lot of pain in my left hip for a number of years which had been diagnosed as osteoarthritis. My GP told me that it was something I had to live with as I was too young for a hip replacement and should take pain killers to stave off the associated pain. Not being one for taking these I declined and just got on with it. This went on for five years or so before I felt that I was limping more and finding walking more uncomfortable. I convinced my GP that I felt something more should happen apart from being diagnosed stronger pain killers, which I wasn't taking anyway. He reluctantly sent me for another x-ray and when I went back to see him for the results, he admitted that it showed a significant deterioration of the joint and referred me to a specialist at the hospital. I subsequently saw a very nice orthopaedic surgeon, Mr Mahaluxmivala. He said that of course I needed a new hip and that he had replaced hips on much younger people than me.

So, on 1st May 2013 I had a new hip. I was asked if I wanted to be put to sleep completely during the operation or just have an epidural so that I would be conscious but feel nothing below the waist. I opted for the latter and so I had a large needle pushed into my lumber region to insert a catheter in order to inject the numbing fluid into my spine. After about fifteen minutes I was feeling nothing in the lower part of my body so was wheeled into the operating theatre. I could feel them hammering away and the odd jolt but did not hear any sawing and I think I must have nodded off for a while. However, I did have view of the clock on the wall and it was exactly two hours later that I was the recipient of a new ceramic hip. I had none of the ill effects of coming round from a full anaesthetic and was sitting up in the recovery room eating toast and drinking tea within minutes. The following day I was out of bed and given a Zimmer frame to use for trying to take my first steps. Apart from the bruising and slight pain from the assault on my left hip I was in no pain from the hip as before. The following day I was given crutches and was hobbling up and down the ward in no time. After demonstrating that I could negotiate stairs using the crutches I was released home. I was given a leaflet giving me some physiotherapy exercises to follow over the coming weeks. After a week I was down to one crutch and after two weeks I was using a walking stick. I was told that it would take full year to get back to full fitness, which turned out to be true. However, what a marvellous relief after years of suffering and I owe a great debt of gratitude to Mr Mahaluxmivala and his team.

Getting back to the training company, there came a time, after nearly five years when things were not running as well as the directors would have liked. They had taken on office premises in Preston near to one of them and another member of staff. The lucrative CKP project came to an end and I got a phone call out of the blue one day from one of the directors telling me that they could no longer afford to employ me. So that was the end of that! I can't say that I didn't feel a little upset about the way it was done considering all the work I had done for them. I didn't have a real problem accepting that my time with the company had run its course but I thought it was handled really badly.

Chapter 24 - Training Consultant - Investigation Company

Very soon afterwards came the Santa job, which lasted from November till the 24th December. I mention this elsewhere so won't talk about it here.

On 9th January 2015 as the result of a phone call from an old mate (Colin), I attended a meeting with the directors of an investigations company. This was set up again by retired senior detectives only these were all ex cadets whom I had joined with back in 1968, in fact, Paul was the one I was at school with. This was primarily an investigations company dealing with corporate investigations for private clients. After another meeting I subsequently agreed to assist them with setting up training courses where they identified clients who may need some training for their staff.

Paul informed me that he had found out the latest information about one of our old teachers at Albany. Apparently, the games master who I had held responsible for losing my grandfather's watch some 50 years previously, had been arrested in July 2015, 30 years after sexual assaults on two boys at the school. He was imprisoned for five years. So, he got his just deserts in the end. He should have taken greater care of my watch shouldn't he! As I have said before "What goes round comes round."

Before commencing any work with them however, Barbara and I went on a Caribbean cruise arriving back in the country on 9th February 2015. Shortly after arriving home our daughter, Kyri, showed us an advert in the local paper for houses being built in Norfolk. She suggested that if we sold our house, we could get one big enough there for us all to live in. It had not entered our heads to move from Broxbourne and thought that we would be spending the rest of our time there. The seed had been sown though and we said there would be no harm in having a drive out one day to have a look. Stuart and his wife together with two of our grandchildren were already living in Norfolk so we were used to the journey there. We visited the show house on the half-built estate and were very impressed with it. None of the houses that were being put up for sale at that time were built yet and so we were just looking at plans. After more visits and discussions, we ended up putting our house up for sale to see how much it would fetch. Unbelievably it sold within a week for a good price and so we were committed to the move. We ended up buying a 3 bedroomed detached property and Kyri bought the one next door. On August 4th 2015 we moved into our new house in Norfolk after 42 years in our Broxbourne home.

The investigations company was a great organisation to work for and treated their workforce very well. I remember that some years previously when I was working for the London agency they invited me to join them on their annual outing to the varsity rugby match at Twickenham. I met up with them at a hotel from where we went to a pub for a few beers before going to the match, where we consumed more beer. During the course of the day I was spoken to by all 3 directors about doing work for them. More drinks were consumed before we eventually retired to our rooms. It was a great day out and I was embarrassed and remorseful that I turned down their offer at that time due to being happy where I was earning a good salary.

When I did start working for them, I was invited to two of their Christmas functions in Cambridge where we were again put up in a Hotel and wined and dined at a local restaurant, which they had taken over for the night. I also attended two of their summer events at Newmarket races, where they provided bottles of champagne to accompany the picnic before entering the ground, champagne inside the grounds and then an overnight stay in a local hotel.

Workwise, they had been dealing with complaints relating to driving instructors and it was identified that there was a training need for this group of people in safeguarding issues. I formulated two 4-hour training programmes. A level one course for driving instructors and a level two course for managers and supervisors. Both of these were fully ready with all supporting material for trainers and students including lesson plans, aims and objectives, power points, time tables, case studies, trainer notes and reference material. I had got both these courses accredited by a reputable awarding body to qualify for the Continuing Professional Development Programme (CPD).

My second assignment with them was to put together a training programme for the Construction Industry Training Board (CITB) another big client, around fraud awareness. After an initial visit to their premises at Bircham Newton, King's Lynn on 11th January 2016 and several more meetings, I put together a 6-hour programme for a counter fraud level 1 course for personnel working in internet testing centres around the country. Again, this was fully ready with all supporting material for trainers and students including lesson plans, aims and objectives, power points, time tables, case studies, trainer notes and reference material. This course was also accredited by the reputable awarding body and met the criteria to qualify for the Continuing Professional Development Programme (CPD).

I identified a number of suitable trainers and we had a meeting with them in London to provide them with all the material they would need for the delivery of the courses and to meet with the directors.

I don't mind admitting that I was very proud of both of these programmes and felt that they not only provided everything needed for the clients, trainers and students but also received acknowledgement from a recognised awarding body.

I must be a jinx because inevitably the company lost a couple of contracts and there was a change of management at the CITB, which affected the uptake of the developed learning programmes. Work then seemed to naturally dry up and I decided that it was time to close down Trayhorn Training Limited (T.T.L.) I had originally wanted to call my company Trayhorn Independent Trainer Supplying Unique Programmes or T.I.T.S. U.P. for short but I couldn't fit it on a business card!

Civilian Trainer Herts

In the Agency London Office

At a Conference

Skillsmark Award

Me, Fred, Colin

Awards (left to right): Long Service Medal;
Cross Country Eynsham Shield; Bronze Medallion

Chapter 25 – Retirement

When Barbara and I moved to Watton in Norfolk in 2015 I was still working for the investigations company and had an office built in the garden so as to get out of the house and Barbara's hair. It was actually a shed really but sold as a garden office. When the work dried up, I kept the shed as an office and find it a very useful and relaxing place to be, especially when researching and writing this autobiography. As recalled in another chapter, I joined an amateur dramatic group but I also joined a local gym. I was walking into Watton Town one day via a back lane when I passed an old building with a notice outside advertising it as a 'Men's Shed' and that men were welcome to pop in for a chat and a cup of tea on a Monday or Wednesday morning. I told Barbara when I got home and said that I might pop in one day and find out what it was all about.

I did just that the following Monday and met a few men who indeed made me welcome and explained what it was set up for. It sounded a very good idea so I decided to join up. I believe I was approximately the twentieth person to join. John was one of the guys I met and he said that they were having a committee meeting soon and I would be welcome to attend. They were looking for active members to act as a meeter and greeter and someone to organise social events. I was subsequently voted onto the committee and looked to organise a social programme. Since that early beginning I have also performed as a Press Officer and Chairman. The membership has now reached 85. I have organised and been on over 45 outings and held over 33 events. Barbara and I have run several quizzes and she has helped me, together with other members and their wives, on cheese & wine evenings, mince pie and mulled wine mornings amongst others.

Chapter 26 – Tap & Am Dram

Apart from the school plays, the times I had performed the Tommy Cooper routine and generally played the fool after a few drinks, I had not pursued any sort of stage acting or serious entertaining. In the early 90's Barbara and I went along to the local college at Turnford one day where they were holding an open evening to promote different courses. As we looked round the different stalls, Barbara saw one that was advertising a course in, 'Spanish for Holidays'. She put her name down for this but I wasn't so keen and continued to browse the other stalls. I saw one that said, 'Tap dancing for adults.' I approached and said to the woman, "Do you ever get any men attending these?" She said that they did and so I signed up for that. When I turned up on the due date, I discovered that I was the only man amongst a number of older ladies. I did persist with this and although I was terrible at it, I bought myself a pair of tap shoes and finished the course. As I was keen to continue, I joined a local dance group that did adult tap classes. This was the Peggy Winchester School of dancing and again I was the only man.

I joined another Tap group in 1997 getting together at a school hall in Turnford on Wednesday nights. Of course, it was all ladies and was called the Elston School of Dancing. Apart from Gillian, the teacher's daughter, all the ladies were of a similar age to me or older. Most Wednesday evening lessons were aimed towards practice for the annual show that was put on for the parents of the youngsters that were also taught by her. Her adult tappers would perform twice during the show. I tended to be put in the centre of the routines, which made me feel a bit self-conscious. "Malcolm you are the only man so you stick out like a sore thumb and the only place I can put you is in the centre." At one of the sessions whilst we were having a break, I was keeping out of the way while all the ladies were chatting. Elizabeth said, "Malcolm why don't you come and join us?" I said, "I thought you ladies wouldn't want a man present while you were engaged in girlie talk." "But Malcolm you *are* one of the girls" was the reply.

The show was on 11th and 12th April 1997 at Cuffley Village Hall and entitled, *'Twinkle Toes'.*

On 8th May 1998 I was back with the Peggy Winchester crowd for their show at Waltham Abbey Town Hall. Elston's School of Dancing put on another show on three nights 8th to 10th April 1999 in which I again participated. I had a lot of good times with all these ladies and we had some good outings and meals out over the years. Unfortunately, my tap-dancing days were to come to an end as when we were rehearsing for the next show things began to get a bit chaotic. The teacher was discussing costumes with the ladies and I was keeping out of the way because she was getting very flustered. One of the ladies said to me that we were to buy hats for one of the numbers and as I was unsure of what was needed and where to get one, I asked, "Are we to buy our own hats?" She said, "Yes, Malcolm, you are always moaning, I've had enough, in fact I want you to leave." I was so shocked at this bolt out of the blue that I changed out of my tap shoes and began to leave. The teacher's daughter, who I was supposed to do a routine with, said, "Malcolm don't leave, she is just a bit stressed out, she didn't mean it." I said, "I am not going to be spoken to like that no matter what the circumstances." I left, never to return, but did send her a letter expressing my disgust at my treatment and demanding the return of the lesson fees that I had paid in advance. She sent these to me but no apology. Shame, I could have been the next Fred Astaire or Gene Kelly! Having said that, when I look at the tapes of those shows, my performances were more cringeworthy than praiseworthy.

As I was not working shifts in 1999, I was able to commit to evening activities and I had the desire to join an amateur dramatic group and tread the boards. Someone suggested the Hertford Operatic and Dramatic Society, so I contacted them and was invited along to their premises to meet them. They were a rich group with large premises that had rehearsal rooms and a workshop with storage facilities for all the scenery and costumes. They even had a bar. I watched that evening and had a brief conversation with one of the members. A few days later I assisted them to erect the stage seating at the Castle Hall for their current production but I didn't really feel all that welcome and thought that they were a bit 'clicky' so I did not join them. I was telling one of my fellow tappers this at a tap class and she said that she belonged to a drama group in Waltham Abbey and I would be made welcome there. So it was that I went along to the small hall in Waltham Abbey, where the Becket Drama Company met to rehearse. I was indeed made to feel welcome and was given a part in their next production that same evening. In fact, I was given two roles in a production of Red Riding Hood. One was as a citizen in a crowd scene and the other was as a beauty parlour assistant in a slapstick scene with the Dame. My only line was, "A mud pack? I love giving mud packs."

Their next production was, 'Lord Arthur Saville's Crime,' a play written from a story by Oscar Wilde. I was asked by the director if I would like to play the lead role of Lord Arthur as he felt that I had stage presence and would be able to perform the character well. I loved the play and that really sealed my interest in amateur dramatics and comedy roles in particular. In January 2000 the company put on a review style show to mark the centenary and I got to be the compere as well as put together a lot of the script and sketches. As we were singing songs to represent each quarter of the past century, I played four different characters as compere. For 1900 to 1925 I portrayed Leonard Sachs, for 1926 to 1950 I was Max Miller, for 1951 to 1975 I was Tommy Cooper and for 1976 to 2000 I was Bruce Forsyth. After that I enjoyed playing many different roles in another seven productions at Waltham Abbey Town Hall with Becket. Characters included; – Sir Lindsey Cooper in a farce called Uproar in the House, Jolyn Forsyte in the Forsyte Saga, Toad in Toad of Toad Hall, General Von Schmelling in 'Allo 'Allo, Frith the butler in Rebecca, The King of Hearts and the White Knight in Alice in Wonderland and Waldorf Patent Pending in Man Alive. The last of these was about a shop manikin that comes to life and required me to be placed at the side of the stage as the audience was arriving and remain statuesque for nearly twenty minutes until my first line as I came to life.

I had really enjoyed the pantomime we did when I first joined the company but they weren't keen on them and had no plans to do another one. One of the company told me that he had involvement with a pantomime company in Chingford and knew that they were looking for a Dame for their next pantomime. He contacted Nial, the director, for me and I was told that I was welcome to go along to their first reading but they had cast all the parts except for the Dame. I went along and watched as they sat round reading through the script. I have to say that the director was a straight-talking strict character and not openly welcoming. He did ask me if I would read in the part of Dame although he was not looking for someone particularly as one of his ladies normally took this part. I read the Dame character putting on a falsetto voice and trying to portray what a male playing this part would be like. At the end of the read through there was general talk and I got to chat to some of the cast members. As they started to leave Nial came up to me and asked me what I thought of the script. I told him I thought it was really good and very funny. He said, "So would you be interested in the part of Dame then?" I said that I would and he said, "Right then you've got the part." So, I got to play my first Dame, Dame Trott in Jack and the Beanstalk for Pinnacle Productions at Chingford Assembly Hall, East London and I loved it!

In May 2003 it was back to farce at Waltham Abbey when I got to say, "I'm Free," as Mr Humphries in a production of *Are you being Served?*

My Dame couldn't have been that bad because Nial asked me to play the part again the following year. This time he wanted me to have an Irish accent as Nanny Murphy in a production of *Sleeping Beauty*. The following year I asked if I could play the villain by way of a change and a challenge. As they were doing a production of *Peter Pan*, I got to play Captain Hook.

Unfortunately, Nial decided that he was going on an extended trip after that performance of Peter Pan in 2005 so Pinnacle productions was no more and I would miss my favourite pantomimes. So, back to Becket and a production of *'Arsenic and Old Lace'*, where I got to play an eccentric character called Teddy 'Roosevelt' Brewster. In 2008 one of the members wished to put on a comedy play that he had written called, *'Oil Well at Endswell'* set in a hospital. It was not the greatest script and was a bit silly but still enjoyable to do. I played the hospital manager who had to dress up at one point as a female nurse (So back in a dress again!).

Directly after this production I was contacted by an old member of Becket Drama Company who had moved to another company after a bit of a fall-out with others. He said that his new company was The Cuffley Players and they were struggling for male members so that they could put on a production of *'Deliver us from Evil'*. I now had another group to add to my résumé and another lovely bunch of people. Although it was a crime play and not a comedy, the character I portrayed was quite humorous so enjoyable to play.

During the summer of that year I got a phone call from a lady who had been the costume mistress for Pinnacle Productions. She had now got a position with another group, the Woodford Pantomime section of Woodford Operatic and Dramatic Society (W.O.A.D.S.) in Woodford Green, Essex and said that they were looking for someone to play an ugly sister in their next pantomime and she thought of me. I attended an audition round someone's house where they asked me to sing to a piano accompaniment. Even though my singing ability leaves a lot to be desired I did get the part of an ugly sister alongside their resident Dame. I was Rubella and this rekindled my love of the part of Dame and also of pantomime. Again, I must have put in a reasonable performance as the following year I was selected as Widow Twanky in a production of, *'Aladdin'*. This Dame is probably the ultimate one to play and I will always remember it with fondness.

That was in January 2010 and shortly after there was another piece of luck for me when my local drama group, 'The Hoddesdon Players', were looking for a male to play a part in their next production so I got to audition for them. They were doing a production of, *'No Sex Please – We're British'*, a farce from the 1970's that sparked the career of Michael Crawford as Frank Spencer. I remember going to see this in London and the character he played was Brian Runnicles who was the epitome of Frank Spencer. Unfortunately, I didn't get to play that role but I had a leading role as a bank manager and it secured my place as a member of another great group of people. Exactly a year later I had a call from my old friends at Becket Drama Company in Waltham Abbey. They were looking to put on a production of, *'No Sex Please – We're British'*, and needed another male person before they could cast it. This is probably the foremost reason why I got parts with so many companies, but who cares, I never said no. Oh, joy of joys this time I was cast as Brian Runnicles and gave it my best Frank Spencer impression (Well sort of!).

In December of that year I was back with the Cuffley Players in my second appearance in *Rebecca* only this time playing a different character. Again, although a serious play I had a humorous character to play so that I could be amusing.

The Hoddesdon Players had a tradition of putting on a sketch and song-based show for friends and relatives of the company. These were great fun and I got to dress up and play several characters in some really funny sketches. That took place in February of 2012 and I was to perform in three more productions that year. Firstly, another show with Hoddesdon players called *Ten Times Table*, a truly hilarious play based on a committee preparing for a festival. Next was *'Witness for the Prosecution'*, a courtroom drama by Geoffrey Archer. Not one of my favourite plays and I opted to just play a prison officer standing next to the dock during the courtroom scenes. That was also with the Hoddesdon Players.

Later that year I was back to the Cuffley Players for a comedy called *Local Affairs*. I played the man in the white suit and to prove it was a true farce I had to lose my trousers. In February 2013 there was another Hoddesdon Players sketch show for friends and relatives following the same format as the previous year.

Hoddesdon Players then decided to put on a production of *'Lord Arthur Saville's Crime'*, another play that I had done before. This time I got to play the mad cap German anarchist, Herr Winkelkopf, who was employed by Lord Arthur Saville to bump off his relatives. This is a great character part and a chance to put on a truly outrageous German accent. One of my favourite shows and one which I think stands the test of time even though it is set in the 1890's. In June that year the Cuffley Players decided that they should put on a show similar to Hoddesdon Players sketch show and apart from other sketches, out came Tommy Cooper again. I have to say that I wasn't so sure that it went down a storm this time, although I did get quite a few compliments.

Back to the Hoddesdon Players in November of 2014 for what was to be my last production before moving to another part of the country. This was a great dark comedy called *'Wife After Death'*, and revolved around the death of a famous comedian. In the first act there was a coffin on the stage and in the second act an urn containing ashes. The character I played was supposed to be the comedian's best friend and script writer. Myself and my on-stage wife were on stage for the whole time and there were a LOT of lines to learn. That company presented an award at the end of each production and on this occasion, I shared it with my 'wife', for our monumental efforts in remembering all our lines as much as for our performances.

In August of 2015 Barbara and I moved to Norfolk so sadly I had to leave all my wonderful Am-Dram. pals behind. When we arrived in Norfolk, one of the first things I did was to check if there was a local drama group and I am pleased to say there was one that had a Website and a number to contact. I rang the number and spoke to Richard of the Wayland Players. He told me that they were holding a meeting round someone's house the following Tuesday and I would be welcome to attend. This I did only to find out that he had told me the wrong day. However, the lady (Jenny), whose house it was invited me in and we had a good chat. I subsequently joined the group and had a new set of good friends. That November I appeared on the local Queen's Hall stage in a production of, *The Game's Afoot'*, a spoof who-done-it comedy based on Sherlock homes. This was closely followed by another sketch show for friends of the group as a Christmas Party event and no, Tommy Cooper did not make an appearance!

Since then I have appeared in another eight productions, mostly farces or comedies. Performances included: -

- *Heatstroke*, when I played a has-been actor Howard Booth

- *Tons of Money* a farce in which I played a character called Henry.

- *That's Entertainment*, a review show with songs and sketches and yes, Tommy Cooper did make an appearance!

- *Kindly Keep It Covered*, another farce in which I played a character called Sidney.

- *Season's Greetings*, a farce in which I played a character called Bernard.

- *Wife After Death*, this was one I had done before with Hoddesdon Players and one that I suggested. I also ended up playing the same role, something I hadn't done before.

- *The Wind in the Willows*, spookily enough although a different name I got to re visit my role as Toad.

Before finishing this chapter, I must say a thank you to a couple of people for motivating and encouraging me in my dramatic journey. Firstly, my English teacher Mr. Barnes who was a real inspiration in my formative years. Secondly, my sister Moira, who has always encouraged me and praised me throughout the years. She actually sent off to opportunity knocks after one of my Tommy Cooper performances. I received an application form to fill in but I never felt confident enough to send it off. I think she has been to the majority of the plays and performances I have appeared in over the years. She has got me to perform at her charity shows and even her wedding reception.

Chapter 27 – Santa

After the training company told me they no longer required my services at the end of 2014, I wondered what I could do to keep me occupied. Looking through the local paper one day I saw a picture of a Santa with the words 'Jolly Gentlemen Required'. I thought, 'I could do that', so I rang the number given and spoke to a man at the Springtime Nurseries in Crews Hill, Enfield. I agreed to go to the Nursery to meet him, view the set up there and talk about the role. On my visit I was surprised at how organised they were and geared up to deal with large numbers of visitors.

They had a large area of the premises decorated as a winter landscape with animatronics and winter scenes. A tractor and trailer disguised as a train with a carriage took the children around the display and at the other end stopped at a station. There was a light signalling system at the station which told the elves which grotto was free. The Santa would press a button at the end of each visit to indicate that he was free to take the next visitor. Elves would then take each child along a coloured line to the correct grotto, of which there were nine in total. The grottos had a sleigh in which Santa sat with a seat in front for the children to sit and all around the room there was a selection of toys to suit all ages and gender. Aaron, who interviewed me and was the person in charge of the operation told me to give it a try and see how I got on.

So, on 27th November 2014 I had my first performance as Santa or as I preferred, 'Father Christmas'. I was broken in gently and saw 51 children on my first day but on the second day it swiftly went up to 125. Average time expected for each visit was 4 minutes and there was no set script. You were expected to ask, "What do you want me to bring you for Christmas?" and, "Are you going to leave something out for me when I come to visit you on Christmas Eve?" Well they were on my list as well as others, such as, "What is on your wish list for Christmas this year?" "Have you got a chimney for me to come down?" "Shall I leave your presents under the tree like last year?" "Will you leave out something for me and my reindeer this year?" It is really a question of engaging with the child or young person who is in front of you. You have to have a quick mind in order to answer awkward questions. "Are you the real Santa Claus?" or "Can you make my Dad well for Christmas?" are just two but there were many that required quick thinking and a considered response. Visitors were not restricted to small children and I had visitors of all ages. One day there was a group of women who wanted to visit Santa as one of them had never done so. I found the secret of success in these instances is to remain totally in character. I said, "Well tell me what you would like me to bring you for Christmas this year?" The group left happy. You could take a break halfway through the shift but by the time you got all the costume off, walked to the refreshment portacabin, walked back and changed again, this only amounted to about half-an-hour. Come Christmas Eve I had seen over 1,500 visitors, mostly children but also some older with a lower mental age. After getting changed on Christmas Eve there was a bottle of brandy presented to each of us for our hard work (which it was).

Unfortunately, I couldn't go back the following year as I was committed to work with the investigations company and the fact that we moved to Norfolk in August of that year. It wasn't until early 2017 that I thought about where I could perform as Father Christmas once more. Ronald, my son-in-law had a job working in a Restaurant at Centre Parcs situated at Elvedon Forest in Suffolk and I asked him if they might be looking for a Santa. He came back with the information that if they had vacant posts anywhere on the complex then it would be on their Website. I checked this out and lo and behold they were indeed asking for applications for a Santa. I duly filled in the on-line application and was asked to go to the centre for an interview. I was seen by two people who had responsibility for the Father Christmas set up and after a few questions I was told that subject to a DBS check I would get the job for November and December. Surprisingly for such a large organisation it wasn't as big an operation as Springtime Nurseries with only 3 grottos in a smaller outbuilding. Having said that, the place was transformed into a Winter Wonderland which was magical for children and adults alike. I met up with the other Santa's who had all done it before, some for a number of years. One even had grown his own beard and certainly looked the part.

The children would be shown in by an elf, who would then prepare a present from a storage area behind a curtain outside the grotto whilst I was talking to the child. The Grotto was decked out with a decorated and lit tree with plenty of fairy lights around the room and decorations to make it look magical. Here, for a one-off payment, the child would get to speak with Santa, have a photo taken with him and receive a present from him. I liked this process better than before. Although the rooms were small, they could accommodate anything up to 20 people at a push and I had photos taken with that sort of number more than once. You might have one child with one parent, one child with two parents and four grandparents or any number of children with any number of relatives and friends. You never knew just what was coming through the door. Although the person in front of you was the most important, I found it essential to also play to everyone in the room. That way everyone left happy and had enjoyed the experience. I saw several children and adults with disabilities and found it very rewarding when making a connection with them and seeing their happy faces.

I have had many mothers and grandmothers in tears watching their children and grandchildren have the Santa experience. I asked one 10-year-old girl what her Christmas wish was and she said, "I would like all the sick children in the world to be well." She was very sincere and an absolute delight, I was nearly in tears myself when she left. To be fair nearly all the children that came in were lovely. I suspect that before they came in, they were right little monsters and likewise when they went out again.

I kept a count of all the children that came in to my grotto and in 2017 I saw 1,722 and that does not include the others that came in with them, if you counted them it would come to over 5,000 easily. That year they had a parade once a week where Santa would walk through the village in the evening after the last grotto visit. Being the new boy, I wasn't included in this duty apart from once later in December when I was given a trial. As a result of that first attempt, I was asked to do the premier parade held on Christmas Eve. For this one Santa would arrive at the entrance to the village on a sleigh, which was a carriage decorated to look like a sleigh and pulled by the centre's horse. There were hundreds of people in the village, lining the way and with the help of the elves I slowly made my way through ringing a hand bell, engaging with as many people as possible, having selfies taken and shouting, "Ho, Ho, Ho" and "Merry Christmas!" every few steps.

I enjoyed this so much that I went back in 2018 and 2019 seeing 2,023 and 1,741 children respectively. I must have done a fair job as I was asked to do the final parade again for both years. It is difficult to describe the joyful feeling I got from doing this, especially the faces of everyone coming into the grotto and the positive feedback from them. I had one grandparent pop her head back after her grandchild had left and say, "Thank you, you are the best Father Christmas we have ever seen." I received many comments like this over the three years I have done it at Centre Parcs so far.

Red Riding Hood

Lord Arthur Saville's Crime

Right: General Von Schmelling –
Allo Allo

Max Miller

Jolyn Forsyte

Sir Lindsay Cooper

King of Hearts

Frith the Butler

Dame Trott

Toad

Mr Humphries

"I'm Free"

Dame Murphy　　　*Captain Hook*

Nanny Murphy

Teddy 'Roosevelt' Brewster

Bank Manager No Sex Please We're British

Hello Mudda, Hello Fadda

Ugly Sister Rubella

Waldorf Patent Pending

Hospital Manager – Oil Well at Endswell

The White Knight

Rebecca

Narrator

Tarzan sketch

Man in the White Suit

Herr Winkelkopf

Ten Times Table

Sketch

Deliver us from Evil

Tommy Cooper

Right said Fred

Widow Twanky

Professor Moriarty – The Games Afoot

Brian Runnicles

Harvey Barrett – Wife After Death

Frenchman sketch

Harvey Barrett – Wife After Death

I'm Getting Married in the Morning

If I were not upon the Stage

Henry – Tons of Money

Howard Booth – Heatstroke

There Ain't Nothing Like a Dame

Prison Officer – Witness for the Prosecution

Sidney – Kindly Keep it Covered

Dirty Fork Sketch

In the Box

I Know My Place sketch

Toad, Ratty, Badger, Mole

Bernard – Seasons Greetings

Springtime Nurseries 2014

Center Parcs – 2019

Chapter 28 – Thanks

My story would not be complete without paying tribute to my family. Barbara has been a wonderful wife, Mother, Aunty, Grandmother, Great Aunt, cook and homemaker. I tell people that we have never had a row in over 47 years and if you asked her, she would say the same. Well she had better or there is going to be a row! One thing that is in common with my children is that they are very good at overcoming adversity and getting on with whatever life throws at them.

Kyri has had a failed marriage and decided to get away from things for a while. She applied for a job on a cruise line and worked in a retail shop on board for a number of trips. She met and became romantically involved with a bar steward from the Philipines. After returning home she asked us if we wanted to go on a cruise. Barbara guessed that she and Ronaldo intended to get married when she joined the ship, so we went with her on a cruise. The journey to catch the ship was a nightmare involving delays due to pilot illness, weather problems, missed connections and the ship sailing before we arrived. However, we did catch up at the next port and had a great cruise during which Kyri and Ronaldo were married on a beach in St. Thomas British Virgin Islands on 31st December 2001. Kyri returned home with us but Ronaldo had to finish his contract. There were difficulties getting him a visa so it took many months and a court appeal to get him entry. For some time, they struggled to have a child. However, they had a daughter, Ellie Rose, on 5th September 2004. Kyri worked hard to train for and secure a job as a dental nurse.

Mark is a very talented individual who has always worked diligently at whatever he does. He has always had a penchant for the finer items in life. I know he would cringe at me telling this story but I remember when he was about 13, he asked for a pair of Nike trainers. I said that they were too expensive and if I got them, he wouldn't appreciate it. He said that he would never forget my generosity if I got them. I told him that I wanted that in writing. A short while later I was given a scrawled note which read, 'I will never forget my Dads generosity', which he signed. He got the trainers and I have kept the note just to remind him now and then. At the end of his school years he decided to apply for a course at University and ended up on a six-year course to study to become an Architect. Five years of this were spent at Manchester Metropolitan University and a year of practical work experience in an Architects practice. He did struggle with the intensity and sheer volume of information and on one visit home I told him, over a pint at the local pub, not to stress about it and if he felt it wasn't for him or was too much to take in, he should jack it in and look for something else. I know that he was thinking that he would be letting us down but I assured him that he wouldn't be. However, he stuck at it and finished the course. He was unable to get a paid job at an architect practice for his years practical experience but managed to get an unpaid post at a practice in Manchester. He got all of his qualifications and was now a fully-fledged architect. The practice where he did his years' experience, took him on as a junior and he worked hard for them for over 24 years, being involved in some prominent building projects. He and some other members have now taken over the practice from the retiring owners and so he is now a director. His wife, Julia, is the practice office manager and gave birth to our grandson, Charlie on 11th December 2007.

Stuart had always found that things came to him fairly naturally and probably didn't have to work so hard to achieve. After school he decided to go to Nottingham University to study a 3-year course in Food Science and Micro-Biology. Whilst studying he developed Myalgic Encephalomyelitis (ME) or Chronic Fatigue Syndrome and was finding that he was spending a lot of time laid up with no energy. With the help of his class mates he was able to finish the course and get his degree. He became familiar with computers and decided to follow a career path in this field.

I was working in the exam section at that time and we were using a trial computer software programme to create and mark exams. The rep from the software company was making frequent visits to our office in Hendon and I was chatting to him one day about Stuart wanting to get involved with things computer. He gave me his number and told me to get Stuart to call him. Stuart did just that and ended up working with the company. Subsequently he moved to another software company and from there he formed his own company together with a programmer. He married Dawn on 22nd July 2006 and we now have two more grand-daughters, Poppy born 1st March 2008 and Rose born 12th September 2011.

I am very proud of all my children and what they have achieved. My grandchildren are all wonderful and I love them all dearly.

So, I can say that I have had a wonderful life so far.

Lightning Source UK Ltd.
Milton Keynes UK
UKHW020957261021
392813UK00002B/11